Bluebird Trails

• *A GUIDE TO SUCCESS* •

Edited by

Dorene H. Scriven

Bluebird Recovery Program
Audubon Chapter of Minneapolis

Front cover   Eastern bluebirds   — Lois Nissen
photographs: Mountain bluebird   — Charles Sleicher
                Western bluebird   — James R. Gallagher

Back cover   Eastern bluebirds   — Lois Nissen
photograph:

Frontispieces: Myrna Pearman
                Lois Nissen

Photographic scans: Jim Auer
Cover design: Joan Gordon
Chapter Headings: Jo Ellen Ortiz
Cartoons: Linda Janilla

Published by: Bluebird Recovery Program
                 Box 3801
                 Minneapolis, MN 55403

Third edition, June 1999   ISBN# 0-9639661-1-1

        Shapco Printing, Minneapolis, Minnesota
              Dione Palmer, Consultant

With gratitude to

those many bluebirders

across the land — east, north, west and south —

who have shared their experiences

"On the Trail"

Contents

PHOTOGRAPHS

ix

Foreword

Bluebird! Whenever people saw a bluebird in the past, it was with a sense of disbelief and excitement, because it was such a rare and special occurrence. Now bluebirds are being seen with increasing frequency, and thousands of people across the continent have discovered the personal satisfaction of helping these beautiful birds survive.

The recovery of the eastern bluebird is a wonderful wildlife success story. That has stimulated thousands of citizens to begin conservation efforts — not only for bluebirds — but for all wildlife species.

The successes enjoyed by eastern bluebirders have now generated additional conservation efforts to help in the recovery of mountain and western bluebirds.

Don't forget — keep it fun, and try sharing the joys of your bluebird trail with the children in your life.

Carrol Henderson
Supervisor, Nongame Wildlife Program
Minnesota Department of Natural Resources

1

2

Preface

Preface to the First Edition:

Do bluebirds need our help? Why a little book on bluebird management? Ask any bluebirder, but be prepared — find a comfortable chair before you do! There's no turning around, for you've entered a world of infectious enthusiasm, nonstop experimentation, perpetual commitment. Our undisguised attempt herein is to lure you similarly down the bluebird trail, strewn here and there with some stark uncontroversial facts interspersed with very biased but no less positive opinions on how to have *the* most successful bluebird trail ever monitored!

More seriously, this volume is also intended as a base of exchange — a collection of suggestions and tricks that have worked and have been passed on by experienced bluebirders anxious to share their ideas.

We cannot emphasize strongly enough — and you'll find reminders as you progress — that while there are some positive *don'ts*, every *do* should be understood to be followed by the word *try*, for there are no absolutes, no two bluebird trails in which all the circumstances are alike — habitat, placement, mounting, nest box, food source, predation. Even if all the physical factors could be duplicated, bluebird behavior (we'll try to refrain from using the word *personality*) varies from the timid young male or female that easily gives up, to the aggressive male or female that will valiantly try to defend its nest from all would-be predators.

We hope this guide will help solve some of the dilemmas of the more experienced bluebirder frustrated by problems, will answer many questions of the novice bluebirder, and will entice those who had never even thought of being "caught' by bluebirds. But be forewarned: once you have attracted that first beautiful devoted pair of bluebirds, you are trapped! Your life will change! You will be beguiled by their beauty, their courtship, and their loving care of their young. The "time you couldn't spare" will be spent watching them, worrying about them, constantly improving your trail, moving your boxes, solving problems, outwitting predators, and boasting to anyone who will listen that you have helped bring "your own" beautiful blue thrushes into a better world!

Preface to the Third Edition

The popularity of *Bluebirds in the Upper Midwest — a Guide to Successful Trail Management* (1988) led to a second edition, slightly updated, and titled simply, *Bluebird Trails — A Guide to Success,* which was favorably received by bluebirders across the continent. Despite some small similar bluebird guides printed since that update (1993), the demand has exceeded expectations, and the sale of all 10,000 copies (both editions) necessitates a third edition.

With the tremendous help of many experienced mountain and western bluebirders, the third edition has been expanded from the original emphasis on eastern bluebirds, to make this guide useful to those fortunate enough to be residing in the upper elevations of the mountain bluebird and the lowlands of the western bluebird.

Acknowledgements

The Bluebird Recovery Program (BBRP) started in 1978 when Dick Peterson, of Brooklyn Center, Minnesota, came to the Minneapolis Chapter of the National Audubon Society for help in answering hundreds of letters which were the result of a comprehensive newspaper article written about his longtime work perfecting what eventually was to become known far and wide as *the* Peterson Bluebird Box. Eleven Audubon volunteers organized the Midwest Bluebird Recovery Program, to spread the word about the potential benefits of " bluebirding."

The Minneapolis Audubon Chapter provided support initially to supplement small tax-free donations received from more and more interested individuals throughout the Midwest and beyond. In 1988 the Minnesota Department of Natural Resources, Nongame Division, provided funds for on-site surveys of 33 diverse bluebird trails in 26 counties. Those comprehensive surveys, added to the hundreds of individual annual trail reports, provided the impetus for the first guide book. Its publication received substantial support, later repaid, from the Nongame Wildlife Funds.

The North American Bluebird Society (NABS), with Mary Janetatos as its Executive Director, 1978-1998, warmly recognized the Midwestern bluebirding efforts. The NABS' quarterly journal, *Sialia*, provided much reference material, especially many articles by founder Dr. Lawrence Zeleny, whose first bluebirds nested in 1918 on the Minneapolis campus of the University of Minnesota.

The Bluebird Restoration Association of Wisconsin (BRAW), and the Iowa Bluebird Program branched off with their

5

own programs in 1986, under the guidance of Delores and Ernie Wendt, and Rita Efta and Jaclyn Hill, respectively. As of 1999, 21 bluebird organizations across the United States and Canada have officially affiliated with the North American Bluebird Society. Others, large and small, are independently organized.

These bluebird programs would not exist were it not for volunteers — many, many volunteers, from the individual who carefully observes a single nest box in the yard to those with several hundred boxes organized into well-designed trails; from the inner-urban database collector, to the busy farmer (who often gets "hooked" himself) allowing strangers access to his land to put up nest boxes, to the retired business person or professional who has leisure time and loves carpentry.

A list of individuals active in the Minnesota Bluebird Recovery Program would be long, but some of the special people include: Vi and Dick Peterson, whose unbounded enthusiasm and love of bluebirds initially infected many of us (and whose exceptional photography graced the first Minnesota Nongame Wildlife Poster). Conservationist Mary Ellen Vetter, retired educator and oft times president of the Minneapolis Chapter of National Audubon, took over the BBRP chairmanship 1986-1991, vastly improving its organization and outreach. Jan & Dave Ahlgren tirelessly continue to construct and ship Peterson bluebird nest boxes, kits and accessories all over the continent, and beyond, besides graciously hosting many BBRP committee meetings. John Thompson, also a photographer, rarely refuses a request for help, whether writing and answering letters, giving workshops, or helping people on their bluebird trails. Ernie & Delores Wendt have for years made the four-hour round trip from Wisconsin to attend our meetings and share their knowledge. Marlys & Dick Hjort from Chisago City have attended bluebird meetings all over the continent, their mini-van packed with promotional material, special bluebird items, plans, and nest boxes.

ACKNOWLEDGEMENTS

Carol and Dave Fiedler of Buffalo, who have, respectively, Master's Degrees for research on tree swallows and bluebirds, share their continuing extensive field research at our annual meetings and through correspondence.

Each of the BBRP Committee members has contributed in his or her own way: Arden Aanestad, Craig Andresen, Dick Eide, Wilma & Art Craigmile, Ken Darling, Dick Eide (who volunteered to proof these final pages), Steve Gilbertson (creator of the Gilbertson PVC box and the Universal Sparrow trap, among other successful inventions), Jack Hauser, Carrol Henderson, Supervisor of the Nongame Wildlife Division of the MN Nongame Program, Pete and Jackie Meyer, Ruth Ogren, Keith Radel, Delores & Ernie Wendt, LeVerne Williams, Melissa Winn and Bruce Wollmering,OSB. Without these BBRP Committee members this third edition would not be possible.

Lois Nissen, a former Minnesotan now in Wisconsin, generously donated her considerable photographic talents to the covers of each of the three editions, in addition to many photographs within. Bob & Lyla Smith of Shakopee, who know their returning bluebirds by name, held spring workshop/field trips for many years. Linda Janilla of Stillwater designed our bluebird logo and arm patch, perfected the Bluebird Banquet keeps us supplied with cartoons and suggested changes for this third edition. Jo Ellen Ortiz (formerly Warolin) has contributed her artistic talent to the chapter headings. Carrol Henderson has been our enthusiastic and essential link to support and recognition by the State of Minnesota. The 1999 Nongame Wildlife Poster features his bluebird photograph and celebrates twenty years of bluebird success. Jim Auer, of Leesburg, Indiana devoted many hours to preparing and scanning 74 photographs.

The following people answered the call to critique the third edition: Allen Bower, Steve Eno, Steve Gilbertson, Mark Ross, John Thompson, and Melissa Winn.

Although this editor spent her first 21 years on the west coast of California, she was oblivious to western bluebirds then. Luckily we were led to Judith Guinan, a Ph.D. candidate under Patricia Gowaty at the University of Georgia. Judy intensively studied western bluebirds in Arizona for two years, and augmented her research with many good references. She is the author of the section on western bluebirds in the forthcoming new Birds of America. She has generously shared her knowledge with us, as well as providing suggestions for changes in this third edition. We are extremely grateful. Pat Johnston and Brenda McGowan of Portland, Oregon, and veteran bluebirder Elsie Eltzroth of Corvallis, Oregon, have shared their knowledge as well.

We were also challenged to provide information on mountain bluebirds, and for this we are grateful to: Myrna Pearman of Alberta, Canada, and the late Art Aylesworth and Bob Niebuhr of Montana. Myrna, Donna Hagerman of Reno Nevada, Elsie Eltzroth, and Charles Sleicher of Seattle graciously donated many photographs.

John Ivanko and Lisa Kivirist, present Executive Directors of the North American Bluebird Society, have encouraged us in this third edition. Many dedicated bluebirders across the United States and Canada, through e-mail and snail mail, have added so much to our knowledge of all three species of bluebirds.

Lastly, but hardly least, this guide would not be possible without those 500 or more bluebirders who took the time and trouble, each year, for almost 20 years, to send in detailed written reports of their bluebird trails, their trials and tribulations and successes.

Thank you all!

The Bluebird Recovery Program of Minnesota
Audubon Chapter of Minneapolis
Box 3801
Minneapolis, MN 55403

Chapter 1

Introduction

Many people today have yet to see a bluebird. While never as common as the robin, which is also of the thrush family (*Turdidae*), the eastern bluebird (*Sialia sialis*) could be found until the 1930s by the careful observer along roadsides, near farmyards, in apple orchards, and throughout most other rural settings. Scattered woods and trees, wooden fenceposts, and generally open land offered food and housing for this cavity-nesting bird, whose main diet is insects. Before the rapid rise of the house sparrow (*Passer domesticus*), these lovely blue thrushes could even be seen in small towns and at the edges of larger cities—from the East Coast to the Great Plains, from Canada to the Caribbean. Their cousins, the mountain bluebirds (*Sialia currucoides*), normally occupy the higher mountain areas of the west and overlap north and south at lower altitudes with the western bluebird (*Sialia mexicana*).

The so-called improvements made by humans on nature often have turned out to be quite the contrary, and indeed often create new obstacles. The decline of the eastern bluebird can be directly attributed to artificial interference aimed at improving human existence, while inadvertently being detrimental to bluebirds. The introduction on the East Coast of house sparrows (formerly called English sparrows (*Passer domesticus*) beginning in 1852 and European starlings (*Sturnus vulgaris*) beginning in 1880 was disastrous, for house sparrows spread very quickly, and starlings eventually, across the United States and became the bluebirds' worst avian enemies.

9

Potential nesting sites were decreased by the removal of dead trees considered unsightly, in the way of clearing land, or needed for firewood; extensive logging practices compounded the problem. Metal fenceposts became easier to purchase and lasted longer than wooden ones, and potential fencepost nest sites also disappeared. Crop production was increased by widespread — often careless — pesticide use, which also undoubtedly had an adverse affect on bluebird populations.

By 1979 the U.S. Fish and Wildlife Service Breeding Bird Survey reported eastern bluebirds "very rare" in many areas of the Midwest and East, "rare" in other areas, and "uncommon " in much of their original range.

Breeding Bird Surveys for the western bluebird are incomplete and as late as 1994 there was still disagreement as to how much they have declined in their range. Colorado, New Mexico and Utah have seen some periodic upward swings in western bluebird populations, but there are no organized bluebirders there to help. Bluebirders in the Pacific Northwest and in California have started the battle to stem the decline. There are definite declines in California and Arizona, reflecting the effects of habitat destruction. Judy Guinan (1999) has written: "I do not have much confidence... as long as we continue to destroy habitat at our current rate. I would urge every bird enthusiast to commit as much time and effort as possible to preserve what is left."

The range of mountain bluebirds may be less severely impacted by human population and development, but comparative tallies are difficult not only because of their montainous terrain, but because mountain bluebirds tend to migrate up and down in elevation, with less spread north and south.

Not surrisingly, awareness of the eastern bluebird's decline preceded that of the mountain and western bluebird. (It was not until the 'forties that the starlings reached California. At the same time the huge westward surge of human population began that continue to this day.) Concerned people started comparing successes—and failures—in the attempt to reverse the downward plunge. Many individuals started to create artificial housing and declared all-out war on house sparrows and starlings. Federal, and then gradually, state, statutes declared house sparrows and starlings to be pests, without protection.

In 1978 the North American Bluebird Society (NABS) was founded in Maryland under the leadership of Dr. Lawrence Zeleny, a former Minnesotan. In the same year Vi and Dick Peterson of Brooklyn Center, Minnesota, approached the Minneapolis Chapter of the National Audubon Society as various newspaper articles about them fanned increasing interest in their long-standing work with bluebirds. The Bluebird Recovery Program (BBRP) of Minnesota was thus initiated. As of 1999, 12,000 people have received nest box plans and information packets. Membership in BBRP at one time reached 3100 people, in 47 other states as well as Minnesota, in several Canadian provinces, and even overseas.

There are now many independent volunteer state and provincial bluebird organizations. Twenty-one of these are now affiliated under the umbrella of the North American Bluebird Society. (See Appendix) Some of these organizations work with, or are aided by, their own governmental departments overseeing nongame animals. This cooperative devotion to aid the recovery of bluebird populations has been entirely devoid of politics, of personal interests, of pride or grandstanding.

Most of these individual bluebird organizations exchange newsletters and ideas. The newsletter of the North American Bluebird Society , now called simply *BLUEBIRD,* promotes sharing, and publishes original material from across the continent.

Friendly debate between organizations and individuals does exist, of course, over the best nest box, the ideal habitat, pairing of nestboxes, or the superior sparrow trap. This has only enhanced the exchange of ideas and the spirit of cooperation. Hopefully, this book carries on both traditions — sharing old ideas, some controversial ideas, and promotes a challenge for new and better ideas!

Join us!

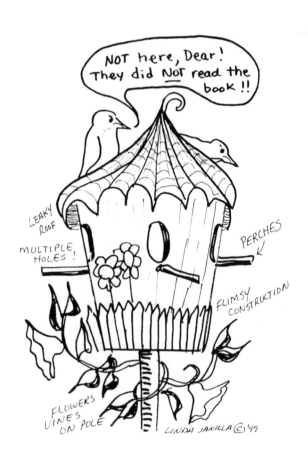

Chapter 2

NATURAL HISTORY

In the last few years, and particularly in the 1998 year of "El Nino", there have been unusual geographic occurrences of all three species of bluebirds. Normally the eastern bluebird is found from southern Canada to the Caribbean and from the Great Plains to the eastern seaboard of the United States. It breeds in these areas, but does not normally winter in Canada or the northern United States. Even after spring arrival, conditions can range from -20°F with prolonged snow and ice in its northern range, to summer temperatures surrounding the nest box of well over 105°F.

The slightly larger mountain bluebird, similar to the eastern bluebird but lacking the red breast, is regularly at higher elevations in the Rocky Mountains from Canada south to New Mexico and Arizona, and in other areas of the mountainous west. It breeds in Western Canada as far north as Alaska. It is an occasional nester in Minnesota, Wisconsin, Iowa, Kansas, and even as far east as the upper Michigan peninsula. In late December of 1998 mountain bluebirds were reliably reported in Nova Scotia, Newfoundland, and several counties of upper New York State.

In 1990, two separate pairs of mountain bluebirds nested successfully and renested in northwestern Minnesota, establishing new state records. Occasional crossbreeding does occur: a mountain bluebird male mated with an eastern bluebird female in Aitkin County, Minnesota, in 1986, successfully fledging five hybrid bluebirds. A similar crossbreeding occurred also in Polk

13

County. The Badlands, Killdeer Mountains, and Turtle Mountains of North Dakota also host mountain bluebirds.

The western bluebird's range, at lower elevations, is from southern British Columbia, and western Alberta, the Pacific states, Idaho, Montana, Wyoming, Utah, Nevada and down through parts of Colorado, Arizona, New Mexico and Texas, and into Mexico.

Several states (Washington, Oregon, Idaho, Nevada, New Mexico and Arizona) can claim both mountain and western bluebirds at different elevations, while Montana, Arizona and New Mexico can go further and claim all three species in parts of their state.

Physical Characteristics

All three bluebird species vary in intensity of color according to season and breeding time. They also, in each species, exhibit size variations influenced by latitude and geography. The male eastern bluebird, $6^1/2$- 7 inches (15.6 -16.8 cm) long, about 28-30 grams in weight, has a bright blue back, forehead, crown, shoulders, wings, and tail. Very faint black and white barring appears in the wing primaries. The throat and breast are rust, with a small white patch at the chin. The rust color continues down the sides under the wings, but the belly is white. The bill, eyes, and feet are black in all three species. A very faint white lower eye ring is not easily visible. The female's front and wing markings are similar, but her blue is quite pale, a gray-blue on the head and back. The posture while sitting is usually hunched, the legs not outstretched. Foraging areas include open low ground cover, lawns, pastures, etc.

The male mountain bluebird is larger, 30 - 31 grams, usually from $6^3/4$ - $7^1/2$ inches (16.2 -18 cm) with a more slender, less hunched appearance. The blue is paler than either the eastern or western bluebird, the chest is pale blue to the white belly. It is

14

thought to hover over the ground more than its cousins, while searching for insects. However, Bryan Schantz (1986) thinks this energy-consuming tactic is used only when there are not adequate perching sites. It frequents high foothills, high valley ranches, open meadows and clearings, sometimes above timberline. It has nested at 11,000 feet (personal observation).

The western bluebird is considered intermediate in size between the eastern and mountain bluebird: 30 grams, $6^3/4$ - $7^1/8$ inches (16.2 - 17.1 cm). It has a slightly longer wing and tail than the eastern bluebird, sports a deeper blue than the eastern or mountain bluebird in the head, rump, wings and tail, and especially characteristic is the deep blue of the throat. The rust color of the breast often extends well over the shoulders. It frequents open, parkland woodlands and scattered oak areas in the foothills to lower elevations.

The juveniles of all three species are spotted in typical thrush pattern, molting into adult plumage in the fall, but retaining the white egg ring for some time.

Albinism

True albinism—white birds with pink eyes—is rare and results in a poor chance of survival, as the eyesight is weak and white birds offer greater visibility to predators. In one recorded case a single albino occurred with normal siblings in both the first and second brood, presumably from the same parents. White feathers in the blue plumage is less rare, and does show up occasionally, making the bluebird remarkable to the viewer, but imposing little threat to the bird. There is no relationship between the occasional white bluebird egg and albinism.

Wintering Range

Banding returns from southern states are insufficient to determine exact wintering sites. Northern-breeding eastern bluebirds are generally found in winter south of a line extending east from southeast Nebraska, through southern Iowa, Illinois, Indiana, Ohio, southeast Pennsylvania (not the Appalachians), New Jersey, coastal New England to Boston. There are exceptions, of course. Small numbers of bluebirds have overwintered in the northern Midwest in recent years. The late Vince Bauldry of Green Bay, Wisconsin, who banded bluebirds for forty-five years, found that his bluebirds winter in western Tennessee, southern Missouri, and Arkansas. Bluebirds banded in Minnesota have been found in Texas, Louisiana, and Alabama in the winter. Due to recent warmer winters and higher bluebird populations, winter ranges appear to have extended further north. In the warmer states the eastern bluebird is a year-round resident. Winter finds the it in warmer climates all the way to the Caribbean and down into northern Mexico.

Both western and mountain bluebirds are less apt to migrate so far south of their breeding range, but are found at lower elevations in the winter. Western bluebirds appear along the coast of California, central Texas, and even into Oklahoma and Kansas.

Banding Records

Although David Fiedler (1974) banded 2400 eastern bluebirds in Minnesota over an eight-year period, nine percent were recovered (a good percentage for bluebirds by national standards). All the recoveries were in Minnesota. (Recovery means the observer was able to read the leg band either through temporary capture or after death.)

People who find banded birds do not always know the significance of the small silver leg band. The number should be sent to the U.S. Fish and Wildlife Service, Bird Banding Laboratory, Laurel, MD 20708, along with the date, exact location, and condition of the bird. Or, call 1-800-327-BAND (2263), or,

16

e-mail: bbl@nbs.gov. Their web site is: http://www.pwrc.nbs.gov/
bbl800.htm. The mortality of first-year bluebirds is fifty percent
or higher, again not unusual for songbirds. The average longevity
for adult bluebirds is probably two to three years; few live more
than five years. The record for mountain bluebirds is nine years
(Schantz, 1986). Zoo-bred eastern bluebirds have lived up to
eleven years of age.

Spring Arrival

Those older eastern bluebirds which breed north of their wintering
range start returning in early March. In the Upper Midwest,
depending on the weather, they may arrive in early March up to
mid-April. A second surge, more likely composed of first-year
birds and depending on latitude and weather, occurs in early May.
Orwin Rustad (1999) has kept records since 1931 in south central
Minnesota. The earliest arrival was February 4, the latest April 28,
with the 68-year average March 17th. Darrell Stave's records in
northern Minnesota indicate an average arrival date of April 3.
Nesting behavior will not begin until several weeks after arrival,
and is somewhat weather dependent. The first nesting peak in
Minnesota, according to Dave Ahlgren (1984) is the third week in
April. In the northeast, people start watching for bluebirds at
maple-sugaring time.

Mountain bluebirds ascend to higher elevations following
snow melt and warmer weather. Western bluebirds which have
migrated may return in March, or even in February, Warmer
coastal areas will attract earlier than the cooler interiors.

Habitat

All three bluebird species have a preference for open spaces with low ground cover. They are not deep woodland dwellers. Before the advent of artificial nestboxes they nested near the forest edge. Secondary cavity nesters, they had to depend on old woodpecker holes, open knots in trees, natural cavities caused by decay or damage. Mountain bluebirds will utilize cavities in fallen trees as well, or even rock crevices.

Bluebirds must forage away from the forest edge where their insect prey on or near the ground is visible. They sometimes had to fly long distances to find suitable food. Artificial nestboxes have helped to provide nesting opportunities closer to the food source, and, with the increase of wren usurpation and predation, especially on eastern and western bluebirds, distance from trees and brush for nestboxes is an advantage.

Pastures, agricultural fields, lawns, cemeteries, burned-over areas, clear-cuts, gravel pits, mowed roadsides, scattered oak savanna - all attract eastern bluebirds if there are nesting opportunities nearby. Western bluebirds like similar habitat, but are also often in transition zones — open woodlands, scattered live oaks, or in small clearings in the foothills and lower mountains; the central Valley of California, largely agricultural. Extensively grazed areas and low meadows attract western bluebirds. In Arizona they may be found in ponderosa pine woodlands and in scattered pinyon-juniper succession areas.

Mountain bluebirds nest in the higher pinyon-juniper areas, on the edges of ponderosa, jeffrey and lodgepole pine forests, and forage out into scree and rocky areas, even above tree line at 12,000 feet. Huge cattle ranches in Montana and Wyoming are prime areas for mountain bluebirds, though perching and nesting sites were often lacking before bluebird nestbox trails were established.

Abundance

Eastern bluebirds benefited from the early clearing of land for agriculture, but then suffered declining populations as trees disappeared, land was developed, and the agriculture turned into agribusiness dependent on pesticides for the best profit. In addition the introduced house sparrow and European starling not only took over their natural nesting cavities, but predated on them as well. Thankfully, the tides have turned for eastern bluebirds. People have learned (to a degree) about overuse of pesticides. Undoubtedly the introduction of man-made nestboxes (and dedicated bluebirders to go with them!) have swung the pendulum up again for eastern bluebirds. Breeding Bird Surveys from 1966 to 1996 showed an annual average increase in eastern bluebirds of 6.9 per cent per year!

According to the same survey, mountain bluebird populations are also increasing in many part of the U.S. with 6.4 per cent annual increase noted in California in the same period. Bob Niebuhr analyzed the reports of mountain bluebird monitors just in Montana over the last 12 years (1987 - 1998). The average increase of reported mountain bluebirds was 11.7 per cent, though there were wide annual fluctuations up and down, mostly attributable to weather. Mountain bluebird populations in Western Canada peaked in the 1940s, and then declined somewhat, but bluebirders in Saskatchewan and Alberta provinces are well-organized to help.

The recent widespread human development in California and Arizona threatens western bluebird populations. The Breeding Bird Surveys 1966 - 1995 showed an average annual decrease of .9 per cent, with a total decrease over the period of 23 per cent in California. A similar decrease has occurred in Arizona. The 1998 breeding season was a brutal one in California with rain and windstorms at the wrong time during the nesting season. The

California Bluebird Recovery Program, founded in 1994, is making tremendous strides toward reversing the western bluebird decline. Bluebirders in the Pacific Northwest have mounted an incredible effort to restore western bluebird populations there. Individuals in British Columbia have a long uphill battle. However, the continued loss of habitat to human development is an increasing threat on the Pacific Coast as well as in Arizona. Most probably the western bluebird will never regain its former numbers in the same manner the eastern bluebird has. Both the mountain and western bluebirds needs more help from more concerned groups and individuals.

Courtship

Roberts (1932) found that "the soft mellow warble of the bluebird, heard at its best throughout spring and early summer, is one of the sweetest, most confiding and loving sounds in nature." Bent (1949) describes the courtship: "The love-making of the bluebird is as beautiful as the bird itself, and normally as gentle, unless interrupted by some rival who would steal his bride; then gentleness gives place to active combat. The male usually arrives a few days ahead of the female, selects what he considers to be a suitable summer home, and warbles his sweetest, most seductive notes day after day until she appears to answer his call. Then he flutters before her, displaying the charms of his widespread tail and half-opened wings, warbling in delicious, soft undertones, to win her favor.

"At first she seems indifferent to the gorgeous blue of his overcoat or the warm reddish brown of his ardent breast. He perches beside her, caresses her in the tender and most loving fashion, and sings to her in most endearing terms. Perhaps he may bring to her some delicious morsel and place it gently in her mouth as an offering. Probably he has already chosen the cavity or box that he thinks will suit her; he leads her to it, looks in and tries to

Lois Nissen

Female eastern bluebird - Minneapolis

Western
bluebird
making
a decision

Merlin S. Elzroth

PLATE 3

Clarence Hagerman

Male mountain bluebird

Jerry Lewin

Western bluebird pair

PLATE *4*

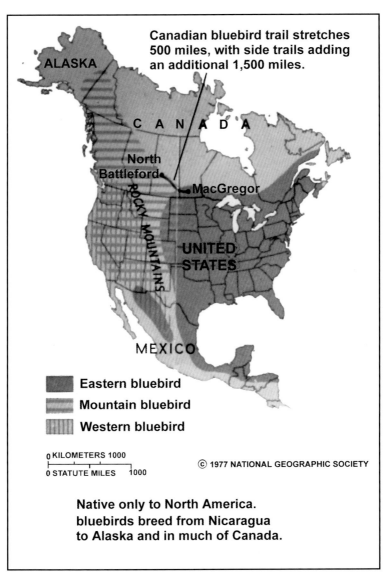

Canadian bluebird trail stretches 500 miles, with side trails adding an additional 1,500 miles.

ALASKA

C A N A D A

North Battleford

MacGregor

ROCKY MOUNTAINS

UNITED STATES

MEXICO

Eastern bluebird
Mountain bluebird
Western bluebird

0 KILOMETERS 1000
0 STATUTE MILES 1000

© 1977 NATIONAL GEOGRAPHIC SOCIETY

Native only to North America. bluebirds breed from Nicaragua to Alaska and in much of Canada.

Distribution Map of Bluebirds

PLATE 5

Female western bluebird

Male
eastern
bluebird

PLATE 6

persuade her to accept it, but much persistent wooing is needed before the nuptial pact is sealed. In the meantime a new male may appear upon the scene and a rough and tumble fight ensues, the males clinching in the air and falling to the ground together, a confusing mass of blue and rust-colored feathers struggling in the grass, but no very serious harm seems to have been done, as they separate and use their most persuasive charms to attract the object of their rivalry. At times a second female may join in the contest and stage a lively fight with her rival for the mate she wants." If a male loses his mate, he seems able to easily and quickly secure another.

Mountain and western bluebird courtship has been less well studied. Western bluebirds are particularly noted during their breeding season for their dawn chorus, beginning before light and ending soon after dawn. During courtship, male bluebirds will hover near , perch on, or repeatedly enter and exit a nest cavity to entice the female. They may make a show of carrying nesting material into it. Often they will offer food, not only during courtship but also, once the female has decided on the cavity and started egg laying and incubation.

According to Gowaty and Plissner (1998) territory size decreases as the nesting season progresses, and also is less in good foraging areas with good perching sites. Territory size also can be reduced by increasing the number of available nesting cavities within an area. Researchers experimentally reduced territory size by placing nestboxes 32.5 feet (10 m) apart.

Studies by Gowaty and Karlin (1984) and Carol Fiedler (1988), indicate that at least one fourth of the eastern bluebirds in one season may switch mates for the second nesting, and even before the first brood has fledged. Infidelity of both sexes, as well as egg dumping by the female occurs (Gowaty and Mock, 1985). Kim Mello, of Wisconsin, who has banded over 2600 bluebirds, found mate switching percentages not that high.

However, extra-pair paternity of nestlings (not all nestlings with same father) is reported common in a California study. Nineteen percent of the nestlings were not sired by the attending male. Egg-dumping by females may occur, but is not common. (Dickinson and Akre, 1998).

With their short life spans, there has to be constant turnover from year to year. Schantz (1986) feels that, at least in mountain bluebirds, pairs nesting together the second year is uncommon. Guinan (1999) states that the 'divorce' rate is low within and between years for western bluebirds, where both partners are still present or return to the breeding site. This is undoubtedly influenced by their minimal seasonal migration.

Nest Site Fidelity

In his eight-year ecological study of eastern bluebirds in Minnesota, Fiedler (1974) found that eastern bluebirds tend to return to the vicinity where they nested successfully the year before, often to the same nest box. First-year birds also tend to return to the area where they themselves fledged the previous year , but often must disperse. In Fiedler's study, 26% of the banded adults returned to the local area, while 11% of those fledged the previous year returned there, and 7% were recovered at least five miles from where they fledged. Delos Dupree (1982) had similar data. Bryan Shantz's study (1986) of 1200 banded mountain bluebirds in Alberta, Canada, yielded comparable statistics: 29% of adult females and 34% of adult males, but only 4 or 5% of immatures fledged the previous year returned the subsequent year. Some yearling males were found fifty to a hundred miles away.

About half the mountain bluebird adults return to successful breeding areas the following year, according to Bryan Schantz (1986), while less than 10% of the first-year birds do.

At Judith Guinan 's (1999) Arizona sites, 61.5% of the banded western males and 46% of the banded female adults returned to the breeding site (not necessarily the same box) in a subsequent year. First-year males were ten times more likely to return to their natal sites than females.

Despite the suggestion of Wayne Davis (1998) that eastern bluebirds preferentially return to boxes where the previous season's nest remains, this is more likely influenced by the location of a successful nesting. Likewise, the returning first-year birds are probably have not been "imprinted" by a particular nest box design, but by the quality and safety of the foraging area, perhaps similar to where they spent their post-fledging time. Guinan found that some of the first-year birds that fledged from her nest boxes in Arizona bred in natural cavities the next year, even though identical nest boxes were available.

Feeding

Unlike tree swallows (Tachycineta bicolor), and violet-green swallows (Tachycineta thalassina), bluebirds are not aerial feeders (but will sometimes snatch a flying insect near their perch). They must be able to see their insect food on or near the ground. Although they sometimes beat low vegetation with their wings to scare up insects, a more typical feeding pattern is that of perching on a utility line, snag, fence post, or exposed tree limb, watching the ground, darting down to the ground or dirt road to catch their prey, then either quickly returning to the perch to eat or flying to the nest to feed their young.

Food includes butterflies, spiders, flies, dragonflies, larval forms of insects (caterpillars), sod grubs, moths, ants, weevils, crickets, small worms, cutworms, apple maggots, corn borers, alfalfa beetles, and so forth. Grasshoppers and beetles are fed to older nestlings. Occasionally, the parent will bring wild fruit such as pin cherries, chokecherries, or raspberries to the nestlings in spring and summer, but the primary food has to be protein.

Many eastern bluebirders, and some Westerners, have utilized mealworms both as a supplement as well as emergency food. Both eastern and western bluebirds, while mainly perch to ground feeders, may also land on tree trunks and momentarily hover over the ground.

Eastern bluebirds may begin eating wild berries as they assemble for their southerly migration in the fall, usually in mid- to late October. Mistletoe and juniper berries are important winter foods for western bluebirds.

Emergency food, which can be offered is discussed in Chapter 8, FOOD.

The Nest

Bluebirds are secondary cavity nesters. They cannot excavate their own cavities. Their natural dependence is on woodpeckers or on rotted out tree stumps, fenceposts, and the like. Cavities of downy woodpeckers (*Picoides pubescens*), hairy woodpeckers (*P. villosus*), red-bellied (*Centurus carolinus*), red-headed (*Melanerpes erythrocephalus*), and occasionally pileated woodpeckers (*Dryocopus pileatus*) are used by bluebirds for nesting. Many other cavity-nesting songbirds also depend on woodpeckers.

With the aggressive house sparrow and the starling taking over these natural sites, it is doubtful how well eastern bluebird could have survived in most areas without the introduction of artificial nest boxes. The mountain bluebird 's habitat, especially at higher elevations, may be less infested with sparrows and starlings. With much of its original habitat gone, the western bluebird's future may also depend on artificial cavities. It is also competing with house sparrows, and since the 1970s, when starlings finally spread to California, those pests as well.

The male bluebird has a delightful song, a melodious warble,

30—40 notes per minute. The gently warbling male will show the female several cavities or nest boxes, from which she will eventually choose one to her liking and begin bringing in nest material. There is some difference of opinion as to whether the male also helps with nest building. One of the many interesting facets about bluebirds is the amazing variation in individual birds. Bent (1949) says both sexes of the eastern bluebird help, though most of the nest gathering and arranging is done by the female, with the male's encouragement, including food offerings. Schantz (1986) says only the female mountain bluebird builds the nest, and apparently this is true with the western bluebird as well. All three species use primarily fine dried grass, formed into a cup-shape by the female's rotation around and around inside the nest, of uniformly small dry grass, without an extra lining of fur or feathers. Some feathers may be present in the nest of mountain and western bluebirds, but a large amount of feathers usually signifies attempted occupation by tree or violet-green swallows.

Judith Guinan often found feathers woven into the nests of western bluebirds in Arizona, in a area without any swallows. Small rootlets, horsehair, may appear, and bluebirds nesting in the vicinity of conifers or cedars may employ needles or cedar bark strips. The chemical composition of pine needles may actually be advantageous in fending off parasites. The size of the nest is determined, to a point, by the interior dimensions of the nest box.

Fiedler observed the smallest eastern bluebird nest in a box of interior dimensions of $3^1/2$" x 4", the largest in one 5" x 5." However, Dick Peterson (1987) found bluebirds nesting in a wood duck box, with the round nest four inches in diameter in one corner of the large box. Bluebirds have also nested in kestrel boxes as well as martin houses.

With favorable weather, the first nest of the season is usually built within five or six days, but maybe built in one or two days if the female is in a hurry to lay eggs (such as when she loses her

her original nest), or it may be delayed over two weeks. The second nest will be built quickly. The depth of the bluebird nestbox may determine the depth of the nest (see Chapter 3 - NESTBOX), though nests built later in the season are often shallower. The top of the nest is usually built so that it is about three inches below the bottom of the entrance hole. Occasionally early in the spring the nest may be built up almost to the hole. The trail monitor should lower the high nest by removing some of the bottom material, but only *after* the first egg has been laid.

Eggs

Contrary to expectation, the size of the clutch is not determined by the internal box measurements. Five eggs is average for the first clutch of a second-year pair of eastern bluebirds.. Six and even seven eggs are found occasionally. A first-year female may have only three or four eggs, and four is not uncommon in the second clutch of both older and younger females. Early clutches of mountain bluebirds may have 5 or 6 eggs, and even up to 8. First broods of western bluebirds have five normally, but more than 6 is rare. The order of the clutches, whether first, second, or even third, can be quite confusing, unless one is observing a single pair of bluebirds almost daily from the time they arrive in the spring. An experienced observer can get to know and identify a particular pair well by subtle behavioral patterns and markings. But positive verification as to whether a clutch is first, second, or third for that particular pair is most difficult unless the birds are banded and recaptured.

One egg is laid each day, usually by midday, until the clutch is complete. The eggs usually range from deep to pale blue. They are oval, weigh about 2.8 grams, and are 7/8" (22 mm) long and 5/8" (16 mm) wide in both eastern and western bluebirds, 22 x 17 mm for mountain bluebirds. As yet no definitive explanation has been found as to why some eggs are white. Fiedler (1974) found white eggs occurred in about one out of twenty nests, but the white color was not necessarily consistent in the same female, nor were her female offspring necessarily genetically predisposed to lay white eggs. Of seven females laying white eggs, only three consistently did so, and one bluebird, hatched from a white egg, was brooding five blue eggs two years later. Four blue and one white egg were found in an Indiana nest in 1988. All hatched.

Incubation

The female does not usually begin the twelve to fourteen day incubation period until the last egg is laid, normally insuring that all hatch at the same time. The nestlings thus have an equal chance of surviving long enough to fledge. The incubation temperature for bluebird eggs is about 95°F (35°C). The eggs are turned and rearranged frequently. Incubation is continuous during the night. Though occasionally fed by the male, the female will leave during the day for varying lengths of time, depending on prevailing temperatures.

Although Roberts (1932) and Bent (1949) indicate the male bluebird has incubated eggs for as much as three periods in one day, Fiedler (1974) found none did. Marilyn Mauritz (1980) of Excelsior, Minnesota, observed certain male birds of other species, notably tree swallows and barn swallows (*Hirundo rustica*), though lacking the female's incubation patch (an area of the lower abdomen devoid of feathers), will stand or squat over the eggs and provide an insulating mechanism while the female is temporarily off the eggs. The discovery by Art Nelson of Long Lake, Minnesota, of a male bluebird dead on five eggs is not uncommon. Male bluebirds not only perform "guard duty" at the entrance hole, but may actually insulate the eggs and even the young nestlings for short periods.

Unincubated eggs may remain viable for some time during cool weather. Occasional cooling of the eggs for very short periods is not harmful, especially during the first week of incubation, but may prolong hatching time. Robert Weidner (1992), a Wisconsin bluebirder and former chicken hatchery operator, writes: "Eggs don't have to freeze to cause them not to hatch. Chilled eggs also will not hatch; when they are not quite chilled to the same extent, they might not hatch but will result in what are called 'sticky chicks.'

"There is a layer of mucus between the shell and the chick that allows the chick to make a complete circle inside the egg in order to peck off the cap of the shell, creating a hole that it can crawl through. Chilled eggs result in the mucus becoming glue-like rather than remaining the slippery substance that it is supposed to be.

"If eggs are chilled, the chick picks a few holes in the cap (from inside the egg) and obtains enough air so that it stays alive, but it cannot make the necessary circle within the egg to peck enough of the cap to exit. It might struggle 4-5 days before it gets out - if it doesn't die in the shell. (The chick doesn't starve in those 4-5 days, because it still has the yolk attached.) This delay in emergence is one cause for uneven size of nestlings with in the brood. The last eggs laid may very well hatch before the earlier, chilled ones, even though all are incubated the same length of time.

"Eggs which have been frozen rather than just chilled will be cracked. Under cool, rather than freezing conditions, eggs will keep very well for two weeks until incubation is started."

Linda Janilla (1999) suggests there is a possibility of saving eggs with fresh minor cracks by (1) drawing a fine line of epoxy just over the crack (2) Using the shell lining white membrane of a chicken egg, wetting the membrane and laying it over the cracks, where it will adhere. These are methods used for rare caged birds owners. This might also work for fresh, small punctures inflicted by wrens when the membrane is not broken, the egg has not lost moisture, the embryo is not damaged, and the parents have not abandoned the nest.

Conversely, extreme heat can accelerate hatching. During the unusually hot months of June and July, 1988, bluebird monitors who were banding nestlings, and therefore handling young from seven to twelve days of age, found many instances of a much wider range of apparent age within a brood, as much as four or five days. The continued extreme heat (in the high 90s to over 100°F) started incubation of the eggs as soon as they were laid. In none of these cases did the apparent age discrepancy affect fledgling time or size at fledging, or success, in contrast to what one expects with raptors, for example, whose young are of different sizes. This is one more indication of how much we have yet to learn about bluebirds. Is it possible the parents in their feeding patterns give more food to the weaker (younger) nestlings?

Infertile Eggs

The cause of infertile eggs is another area needing more research. Dave Fiedler believes lower hormone levels in both sexes are the primary cause of infertility, and the hormonal decrease is keyed to the length of the nesting season: hormone levels peak in May and gradually drop throughout the rest of the summer, evidenced by fewer eggs on the average in the second nesting. The drop may also explain a larger number of desertions of nest attempts into July. "Miniature" eggs, sometimes found in the second clutch, are not fertile. Trauma to either male or female may also be a factor. Immaturity certainly is.

Heavy and prolonged snow cover, and conversely, extreme drought, heat, and subsequent lack of food, can affect the nutrition of both potential parents. The maximum temperature for bluebird egg viability is probably around 107°F (which can happen in some nesting boxes even when outside temperature is only 87°F). In this regard, it should be noted that eggs reported as infertile could instead have been addled (that is, the eggs were fertile when laid, but spoiled sometime thereafter). And there are many causes of addling besides extremes of heat and cold.

Extreme care should be used in handling eggs within the first week, as the shell may still be soft, and rotating or shaking the eggs could cause addling.

Chemicals are known to reduce fertility in raptors, though Dr. Zeleny believed ten to fifteen percent of bluebird eggs are infertile by nature's defect rather than by human agency, such as pesticides. Parents may carry off infertile or addled eggs after the fertile eggs hatch, but more often they are left in the box and remain there uncrushed through fledging. The parents may abandon an entire clutch of infertile eggs and renest or build a new nest over them with a clutch of fertile eggs. The female's awareness of failure is not always immediate. Some abandon infertile eggs after only a few days of incubation, while others continue to incubate past the normal thirteen to fourteen day period. The record may be set by one female who sat on the same eggs for twenty-eight days, while another alternated on two clutches of her own eggs eighty-four days!

About sixty-five percent of all eggs hatch. It was long thought that the female carries the egg shells to some distance, but recent in-nest videos (Pease, 1998) revealed that both the female and male consumed some of the fresh shells in the nest box.

Nestlings

The newly hatched young, weighing just over 2 grams, are altricial (almost entirely naked), with a few bits of down sprinkled on the head and along the spine (see the photographs that follow). Young bluebirds are extremely susceptible to cold and weather changes at this time and are brooded by the female almost constantly until they are about six days of age. Thus, contrary to what one might expect, these very young nestlings seem to survive early cold, damp spells better than the feathered nestlings. As with early eggs, care should be taken in examining very young nestlings. They should be returned in their original position .

During this time the male will bring food to the nestlings and to the female, though she may leave the nest more frequently and actively feed the nestlings during warm weather. By three days, down has appeared on the wing margins and along the spine. After six days the down cover has only slightly increased on the head, wings, and tail, and the nestlings are still mostly bald. Both parents now share equally in bringing small, soft insects about once every five minutes, or about a dozen per hour. Each nestling, regardless of the total number in the brood, is fed two or three times each hour until it fledges, the fare changing to larger insects, such as beetles and grasshoppers, as the nestling matures.

By the eighth day, the weight has increased 10 times, the eyes, which may open as early as the sixth day, actually begin to focus, and the pin feathers break through the skin on the wings and back, supplanting down. The wide areas between the back and wings remain bare even up to nine days, when the pin feathers start turning blue. Development rapidly increases and by the thirteenth day the body is completely covered. The wing primaries turn blue (bright blue in the male) with white edges showing. By this time—when the primaries reach 2" (50 mm) or more in length—it is possible to sex the young. The male's primaries and tail feathers are dark blue, the female's are more dull.

Fecal sacs of very young nestlings are consumed by both parents, The fecal sacs of older nestlings are carried away at some distance.

If predation is not a serious problem, 95% of the nestlings may attain fledging from the first nesting, and 55% (or more) from the second (Musselman, 1934).

Fledglings

An extremely critical time begins after fourteen days. The nestlings can fledge prematurely—that is, they can leave the nest box before they are sufficiently prepared. Because they are still unable to do more than flutter a few feet on the ground, this is an extremely dangerous period. The nest box should not be opened at this time unless there is strong evidence of a real emergency—predation or long absence of both parents. If you have doubts as to whether the nestlings are being fed, put a soft obstruction across the hole— some spider webs, a blade of grass, a tiny twig, a piece of thread— while you finish monitoring your trail. Nestlings can live up to twenty-four hours without food, but an absence of more than two hours by both parents is cause for concern and extended vigilance (see Chapters 5 -MONITORING and 8 - FOOD). If the nestlings respond to the alarm call of the parents and fledge prematurely, they will not return to the nest and it is almost useless to try to keep them in.

A single dead nestling near fledging age (or a living nestling if the monitor is lucky and checks frequently) is sometimes found, apparently because it was unwilling or unable to leave the nest when its siblings fledged.

In summary, *all observation after the nestlings reach 14 days of age should be made by watching the nest box from a good distance.* In reporting fledging dates or success, we must make assumptions, unless we are lucky enough to observe the fledglings leaving one by one as they are enticed out by the parents withholding food and calling to them, sometime between the 16th and 21st day. Guinan (1999) rarely saw her western bluebirds in Arizona fledge before 19 days of age. Bluebirds which have become used to regular daily checking into the nestbox would be less likely to prefledge from fright when the box is opened even near to the 14th day of the nestling period. (See Chapter 5 - Monitoring). Assumed fledging should be reinforced by observations of the vacated nest as soon as activity around the box has stopped. If the nest is vacant, flat, and clean (there may be one or two fecal deposits from departing fledglings), we can assume successful fledging -- and be proud as punch, if maybe a little sad. Any sadness will turn to joy when, after a week to ten days, or sometimes much longer, the still -spotted young accompany their parents out into the open from the comparative safety of nearby trees. They may even assist their parents with feeding nestlings of the new brood, a phenomenon rare in most avians.

The fledglings may fly 150 feet or more on their first flight. The male parent often takes charge of their feeding and protection while the female renests in a matter of hours or within a day or two.

Usually the same pair will stay together for the second and possibly a third nesting of the season. But mate switching, initiated by the male, may occur. Indeed the male may father another brood while the female is caring for the first brood. A brood of mixed parentage is not unusual (Gowaty and Mock, 1985).

The second nesting and laying of eggs, which may begin even before the first brood has fledged, normally peaks in early June in the Midwest. Mountain and western bluebirds, with shorter migration distances, nest earlier than migrating eastern bluebirds, and the second clutch is also earlier. Fewer eggs may be laid the second time, and fewer nestlings may reach maturity. Eastern bluebirds may produce a third brood in a favorable year.

Fall Migration

Bluebird family groups seem to disappear in August and September, moving considerable distances from the nesting area as they forage for food, but then congregate in larger groups in late fall. Later into October hey are frequently seen strung out along utility lines during October. Both young and adult birds sometimes flutter around and go in and out of nestboxes. As the insect population dwindles, the eastern bluebirds turn to wild berries and other small fruits as they start their migration south. Mountain bluebirds will go to lower elevations, for insects and for wild fruits. In most areas of their preferred habitat, western bluebirds will continue to have insects for their main far through their relatively mild wintering season.

Chapter 3

Nest Boxes

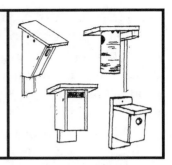

Which is the best nestbox for the eastern, the western, and the mountain bluebird? There is no single answer. What a dull world this would be if we all agreed! Yet many of us happily argue till exhaustion about the perfect nestbox. The only agreement among veteran bluebirders is that the box must be well ventilated (but not too much, especially in the north), well-insulated, especially in the north (but not too heavy), predator-resistant (but what diverse opinion there is on the best predator-proofing!), and easy to clean (but should it open from the top, the side, or the front?)

It must never have a perch (though scratch marks are all right). It must be made starling-proof, but unfortunately cannot be made house sparrow-proof, as sparrows can occupy any nest box a bluebird can.

So should the beginning bluebirder just buy whatever box is marked "Bluebird House" in the discount store, craft shop, garden store, or feed catalog? Absolutely not! Most of these cute or simple houses are mass-produced commercially or turned out by someone who loves woodworking but knows little about bluebirds. They are either inadequate or downright disastrous for bluebirds. Not only are they usually expensive, but what is worse, rarely is any information included about where and how to put up and care for the box.

The only thing that angers bluebirders more than the cheap grocery-store birdseed, which is ninety percent milo or millet and perfect for helping unwanted house sparrows propagate, is the

proliferating sale of bad nest boxes to innocent buyers who want
to help our feathered friends. While it is true that bluebirds will
nest in old boots, bottles, mail boxes, tin cans and badly- designed
boxes if they are in a good location, when we deliberately attempt
to attract bluebirds, we should feel obligated to use a box built to
the best advantage.

Where can we get proper nestboxes? Contact any serious
birding or conservation organization, where the people are concerned about birds, not about profit. Many state and provincial
bluebird organization have plans. The North American Bluebird
Society has several box plans and a nestbox certification of
approval for commercial manufacturers. (See Appendix.)

The Peterson Box

Used by four out of five eastern bluebirders
reporting to BBRP (admittedly because it is
highly recommended), the Peterson box is
slightly more difficult to make for it has
63°, 45°, as well as 90° angles to cut. Its availability as a kit at
the cost of lumber plus shipping offsets this problem. (See
Nestbox sources, Appendix.)

Some individuals have simplified or modified the basic Peterson design, but in so doing have changed the total concept
developed over thirty years of bluebirding by Dick Peterson. The
large (9" x 13") sloping roof greatly overhangs the box front and
sides, providing protection from the hot afternoon sun. The sharp
slant of the roof makes it difficult for a cat or raccoon to sit and
swipe at adult birds or reach into the hole from above. The inside
top and back are constructed of 2x4's that provide insulation and
sturdiness.

The slanted bottom eliminates moisture accumulation and
allows easy nest observation and cleaning. Adequate but not

excessive ventilation is provided by two $^3/4''$. holes in the upper area of each side and the $^5/8''$ space above the entry hole. The oval $1^3/8''$ x $2^1/4''$ entrance is designed for easy access by adult bluebirds. The narrow hole and the small interior discourages starling usurpation. Without an exterior predator guard, an adult bluebird can feed the young and remove fecal sacs by clinging to the outside with head and shoulders extended through the hole rather than having to completely enter, turn around, and exit again.

The small dimensions of the floor of the Peterson box means less nesting material is required at the bottom of the nest than, for instance, in a 5" x 5" square box. (Bluebirds usually fill the box to within three inches of the hole in the Peterson box.) But five, six, and even occasionally seven-egg clutches are no less frequent, nor is fledgling success lower. The swing-down front gives a clear view of the nest. It may be left down during the winter, which effectively eliminates mouse, squirrel and house sparrow use during that period. (Preventing prior claim to the box is an important tactic in dealing with house sparrows.) The slant of the front makes fledging easier, especially for tree swallows, and, easier removal for the parent bluebird if a nestling dies.

The "Peterson system" allows for the addition or substitution of alternate fronts such as the Noel Guard with adapter, the sparrow trap, as well as adaptation of the entrance hole size to fit other desirable birds.

Should a chickadee place its lovely moss-bottomed nest in a Peterson box, the front can be dropped down temporarily and replaced with one having a $1^1/8''$ entrance hole, thereby protecting it from larger birds.

North American Bluebird Society (NABS) Box

 The North American Bluebird Society (NABS) nestbox features either a top opening or side-opening design. It is a 4" x 4" rectangular wood box with a 1 ½" round hole hole, and a slightly sloping narrow roof.

The top-opening version, originally called the Duncan box, allows a clear view of the eggs and nestlings (especially for photography), less potential for the nestlings to fall or jump out when banding or monitoring, safe observation of the nestlings for a longer period of time and with less disturbance to the brooding or incubating female and the nestlings (Grant 1988). However, a box which opens only from the top (1) may be more difficult to keep sealed from rain and snow (unless there is a well-sealed cleat over the roof at the back and the roof overhangs sides and front), (2) does not allow thorough cleaning or inspection for blowflies under the nest, and, more seriously, (3) must be placed low enough for the monitor to see into the box or the observer must carry something to stand on. Low-mounted boxes in pastures may be used as rubbing posts by livestock.

Monitors at the Ellis Bird Farm in Alberta, Canada, use the open-topped box successfully for several reasons: they rarely have blowflies, they not only seal the top cleat with silicone, but add cleats under the roof sides which fit snugly against the box, and they use a floor which pivots open for end-of-season cleaning.

The side-opening version of the NABS box has been used for many years by eastern bluebirders, earning the term "standard box." Mountain bluebirders have expanded the inner dimension to 5 "x 5" and the entrance hole to 1 $^9/_{16}$" for use not only in mountain bluebird territory, but wherever the mountain bluebirds may overlap with the eastern or western species.

The Herman Olson Box

The Herman Olson box , developed in Wisconsin for eastern bluebirds, is similar to the NABS box. The bottom of the entrance hole is $6^7/8"$ from the floor. The slightly sloped roof roof overhangs the front minimally. Inside dimensions are 5" x 5".

The guard over the entrance hole is designed to reduce raccoon and cat predation by increasing the entrance depth. This requires the adult bluebird to completely enter the box to feed the young or remove a fecal sac, then turn around and exit. Zeleny (1976) found that bluebirds tended to avoid entrance holes more than $1^1/2$- in. total thickness if thinner entrances were available. Moreover, the extra thickness at the entrance has not withstood determined raccoons. The deep Hill-Lake nestbox, developed by Andrew Nelson, Wisconsin in a response to raccoon predation, is similar to the more shallow Herman Olson box, but because of its depth, is less often chosen by bluebirds.

A fourteen-year study by David Fiedler (1988) indicates that exceptionally deep boxes may require more nesting material, as may wide-bottomed boxes. Fiedler's data show that nests were constructed of more material (by weight) in larger nest boxes than in smaller nest boxes. Fiedler believes that "bluebirds will attempt, to a point, to fill nest boxes to within a certain distance below the entrance regardless of the initial depth of the nest box. That is, the deeper the nest box, the more material required for the birds to add to the nest to bring it to the required height.''

Slot Boxes

 Many years ago Rita Efta, a prime mover in Iowa's bluebird conservation movement, experimented with a wooden slot box, which had a 1 $^3/16$" slot across the top of the front as the only openingin the box. It attracted bluebirds and seemed less attractive to house sparrows. Wayne Davis (1989) of Kentucky also found a slot across the top of the front was not only used by eastern bluebirds, but was less attractive to sparrows, who seemed to prefer a round hole entrance. There is some question whether a bluebird caught by a house sparrow in a nestbox is more easily able to escape through a long but narrow slot than through a circular or oval hole.

The slot box developed by Andrew Troyer of Conneautville, Pennsylvania, has become a favorite of many people, and is endorsed by the North American Bluebird Society. Allen Bower, veteran bluebirder of Ohio writes: " I favor this box and can see a lot of thought has gone into its design. It is sparrow resistant, because it is compact. The floor is 3$^1/2$" x 3$^1/8$", the depth is 4$^1/4$ " from bottom of entrance to floor tray. The front slants 15° . The under-roof helps insulate from the heat, and discourages house sparrows from "doming" over their nest as they are prone to do.

Troyer also uses a piece of hollowed-out 2x4" "tray" on the floor, into which he adds sawdust. because he believes that sawdust increases the desirability of the box. Care must be taken that this "tray" does not cause the nest to be built too close to the entrance slot. A shallow box may deter house sparrows, but if the top of the nest is too close to the entrance hole, and a mammalian predator can climb up to the box, this would be dangerous for the birds.

Mountain Bluebird Nestboxes

All the boxes mentioned previously have been used success-fully for eastern bluebirds. However the mountain bluebird box should be slightly larger, and the birds may select a slightly larger entrance hole if given a choice. Most mountain bluebirders use a wooden box with at least 5" x 5" interior dimensions, and a 1 $^9/_{16}$" round entrance hole. Bob Wilson, of Grand Junction, Colorado, uses a 1$^1/2$" round entrance hole with considerable success. (Wilson, 1999) One of the first pair of mountain bluebirds reported nesting in northern Minnesota did use a regular Peterson box, but when a second box was added nearby with the oval entrance hole enlarged to 1$^1/2$" by 2$^1/4$" , that box was used for the second nesting.

Whether this was a conscious selection of a larger hole is debatable. Veteran bluebirder Myrna Pearman of the Ellis Bird Farm has observed that if an adjacent box is empty, her mountain bluebirds tend to use it for the second nesting, no matter what the box style. If it is occupied, they will renest in the same box. (Pearman, 1999)

Wherever the territory of mountain bluebirds overlaps with either eastern or western bluebirds, the larger box should be used. It took many years for Art Aylesworth, of Ronan, Montana, and others, to convince the North American Bluebird Society that a larger entrance hole (1$^9/16$") in the standard box was better for mountain bluebirds, yet could not be entered by starlings. Art and some other bluebirders see no reason why it cannot be the standard box for all three species.

Nails or Screws?

Galvanized nails are the cheapest to assemble a nestbox, but they are far less secure over time and difficult to remove for changes. Every bluebirder should be prepared for the eventual necessity of replacing box fronts, roofs, and even sides! Ring-shank nails may be used to close the box if there is no threat of vandalism. Dry wall screws, which come in black or a gold color, will rust, although a dab of silicone caulk will slow the rusting process. Deck screws, designed for outdoor use, come in galvanized, silver or gold color. 1 1/4" deck screws can be used for sides and back, and 1 1/2" deck screws for the boxes with double roofs. An electric drill in the shop, or a cordless one in the field for minor repairs, makes the job easy.

Green or Brown Treated Lumber, Exterior Plywood

Copper arsenate is injected into lumber to preserve it and as a pesticide. Such treated lumber should not be used for animals or birds. Much of the lumber found in lumber yards today has not been sufficiently dried before injection, which means the copper arsenate does not impregnate well. In addition, it may be sold before the two months or more required to sufficiently "set", meaning the arsenate may still "bleed" out.

Required instructions from the producers are rarely followed or passed on to the small consumer: they include wearing plastic or rubber gloves to the elbows, a full face mask and eye protection. No burning of scraps. There is a reason for those cautions: the human body cannot get rid of arsenic. It could be fatal. Animals which may drink water standing around treated lumber may be poisoned. It stands to reason the birds we are trying to protect should not be exposed to it either.

Many exterior plywoods and some exterior sidings (not hard-board) may have a high concentration of formaldehyde, If you are going to use exterior plywood for economic reasons (and you can paint or stain the exterior parts anyway to preserve them), let them "season" outside for a several months before using. Exterior plywood $^3/8$" or less thick in single roofs will become hotter than

^{3}/4" pine, will warp, and not provide adequate insulation. 5/8" plywood should be the minimum thickness.

Economy Boxes

(1) Distressed and damaged materials are available from the lumberyard at a discount or for free.

(2) Small home builders and remodelers often have a scrap pile near the street available for the taking if you ask. (Do not take OSB (oriented   strand board,or chip board, which will deteriorate quickly.)

(3) Dumpsters at commercial buildings during remodeling are a possibility, but may be inconvenient and even dangerous to get in and out of. [Also treatment of the material is unknown—Editor.]

(4) Befriend a carpenter with a pickup or van. He might even deliver to your door!

(5) Keep your eyes open—salvage is the flip side of solid waste, which is everywhere.

Interior grades, and plywood, should be thickly painted or sealed. Siding, especially cedar and redwood can be doubled if not thick enough.   Masonite siding is quite dense but has less insulation value. Western red cedar lumber of the grade used for fencing can often be obtained quite cheaply.

(6) Check at a print shop for used paper pallets, usually made of wide, heavy boards.

Caution: do not change the nestbox design or entrance hole to accommodate pieces of used lumber.

Nestbox roofs are usually the first part to deteriorate. Light-colored shingles can be used over the top roof. Ron Kingston of Charlottesvile, Virginia,   found that a composition concrete-fiberboard, called Hardiplank® makes a good roof. The Bluebirds Across Nebraska organization has endorsed this roof. It is just ^{5}/16" thick. It's insulation value is slightly lower than wood, and wood, and a dust mask or vacuum system should be employed when cutting it, but it has a 50-year warranty against deterioration. Few of us will outlast that roof!

Finishing Wooden Nest Boxes

Cedar, cypress, yellow or tulip polar, PVC and redwood boxes need no finishing, although a waterseal or exterior varnish may be applied (on the outside only). The entrance hole itself should be sanded smooth, but not painted or stained.

Boxes of pine, plywood, or scrap lumber will last longer if painted (outside only), always using a light color— light beige, light brown, tan, green, or other. Where vandalism may be a problem or where unobtrusive appearance is desired, light brown and green or gray camouflaging may be tried. Questions about using wood preservative frequently arise. Fumes of copper arsenate, creosote or formaldehyde are toxic and are given off for some time. Cumulative effects on small birds have not been studied. Always check the warning label on the preservative container. Never coat the interior or the entrance hole with any preservative. A preservative-treated nest box should be left out in the hot sun at least one season before being offered to bluebirds. Linseed oiled wood works well, but does take several weeks to dry.

Plastic Jugs, Milk Cartons, and Gourds

Plastic jugs, milk cartons, cardboard, and thin gourds should NOT be used for bluebird nestboxes. However, at Ellis Bird Farm in Alberta, tree swallows have nested successfully in gourds. Varnished cardboard and milk cartons are easily destroyed by predators and are not weather-resistant. Even with multiple coatings of white latex paint, the inside temperatures have become high enough to cook the eggs and kill the young. Thorough cleaning, removal of parasites, and inspection during monitoring are impossible. (The newer white plastic jugs specially made for martins do feature access for monitoring). Jugs and milk cartons are easily pulled off and destroyed by four-legged predators and two-legged vandals. House sparrows may not like these containers, but that doesn't justify using them for bluebirds.

PVC Pipe Nestboxes

Several people in Wisconsin, Iowa, Minnesota, and Texas have experimented with sections of large PVC (polyvinyl chloride) pipe, usually capped with a wooden roof overhanging the pipe and fitted into the top of it. Its smooth exterior has some advantages in predator protection, especially when mounted on a tall smooth mounting pole.

In 1989 Rita Efta of Iowa wrote: "I have used 6" PVC boxes 10" tall (total height) for the past four years and found them satisfactory and readily used by bluebirds. Because of their light color, they reflect the hot sun and do not take on excessive heat. Of course, 1/2" ventilation holes were drilled near the top. The [wooden] top is easily removed to monitor the contents. The bottom can also be removed to discard old nests. Several holes drilled through the PVC and the top to accommodate nails makes it easy to remove them. It seems sparrows are more reluctant to use them than [they are to use] a wooden box."

Although there is as yet no nestbox that bluebirds will use and house sparrows absolutely will not, they are very reluctant to use the shallow PVC pipe nestbox designed by Steve Gilbertson of Minnesota (1990). When they occasionally do start a nest, they quickly give up when the nest material is removed. Eastern bluebirds have readily accepted the PVC box, and in some experiments have even chosen them over a wooden box. After experimenting with long and short lengths of PVC for several years,

Steve found that an 8" length of 4" PVC, with the $1^1/2$" entrance hole just $4^1/2$" above the floor, was most attractive to eastern bluebirds, used safely by tree swallows, and avoided by house sparrows. The box has produced bluebirds successfully for many years . It is painted on the outside to resemble birch bark and painted dark brown on the inside to simulate a natural cavity. The Gilbertson box is mounted on five-foot lengths of 1/2"(inside measurement) conduit pipe, which is itself mounted over five-foot lengths of 1/2" (outside measurement) rebar (reinforcing bar used in concrete). For extra precaution the conduit should be treated with carnauba wax. Raccoons find it extremely difficult to climb. The box has the approval of the North American Bluebird Society.

Professor Neal Mundahl of Winona State University compared the thermal characteristics of unoccupied Gilbertson and Peterson boxes. Daily maximum and minimum temperatures did not differ significantly. The major difference was in the rate of warming and cooling. In early morning the PVC boxes warm much more rapidly. After sunset, they lost heat more rapidly.

Bob Wilson of Grand Junction, Colorado, uses 1" x 6" PVC white fencing material for mountain bluebirds and found that the PVC was always cooler than wooden boxes. His mountain bluebirds used both types equally.

Anyone experimenting with PVC should be sure there is enough ventilation, that the box easily opens for monitoring, and that there is provision made in any deep PVC box to allow tree swallows or violet-green swallows, whose feet are weaker than those of bluebirds, to exit easily.

Other Designs

The open-topped Bauldry box, used extensively in Northern Wisconsin by the late Vince Bauldry, does discourage sparrows and wrens, but we do not recommended it, nor does the Bluebird Restoration Association of Wisconsin, nor the North American Bluebird Society. Late winter snows and freezing rain cause problems in an open-topped box. There is a considerable difference between a dry, warm nest, and a cold, wet one in the early spring. And, later, a box shading the nestlings or one with blazing hot sun shining down on them.

The commercially advertised "Native America" box, deep, front-slanted, and open-topped, has the same disadvantages.

Several years ago Frank Zuern, in Wisconsin, introduced a "Tree Branch" box in the belief that bluebirds in the past sometimes nested in holes at the ends of tree branches. By making the box narrow and horizontally long, with two baffles inside, he thought there would be better protection from predators, and the box could be mounted on large wooden posts. He has since recommended a smoother mount. These boxes have produced bluebirds, but in trials elsewhere, in high house sparrow areas, the boxes have proven to be especially attractive to those pest birds. Moreover, nestling bluebirds and tree swallows sometimes get over the baffle on the wrong side.

Summary of Nest Box Designs

Both Professor Wayne Davis of Kentucky, and Professor Kevin Berner of the State University of New York, Cobleskill, have done controlled scientific studies to determine which style of several different nestboxes was most often chosen by eastern bluebirds. In each study the Peterson box was determined to be the preferred style.

Professor Berner conducted a six-year study, beginning in 1989 of nestbox preferences by eastern bluebirds. Five different study sites in upper New York State (1993,1995). At each site there were 10 nestboxes each of the Peterson, North American Bluebird Society (NABS), slot boxes and Gilbertson PVC. In the last year of the study, two new research sites were added which included the Zuern Tree Branch Nestbox. Bluebirds and tree swallows showed a strong preference for Peterson boxes, using them at much higher rates. The next highest level of use was in the PVC and slot boxes, followed by the NABS boxes.

Sparrows avoided the PVC entirely. Wrens, present only in small numbers, seemed to have no preference. No bluebirds chose the tree branch box (fewer were actually available) but a few tree swallows did and sparrows were attracted to them; Professor Davis's tests comparing Peterson and tree branch boxes supported these overall findings (1995):

" The fact that Peterson boxes are consistently occupied and rarely vacant for the entire breeding season indicates that the birds see some advantage to this style. An advantage that I have observed is that the downward sloping design tends to result in much drier nests after rainfall. Concern has been expressed that starlings can enter the oval entry hole in Peterson boxes. I observed no evidence whatsoever of this happening at any Peterson box. Relating to house sparrow deterrence, I have found the PVC box to be the most promising design... I highly recommend this box to any one with sparrow problems."

Naturalist Ken Fitz of the Dawes Arboretum in Newark, Ohio, also studied nesting preferences in 18 boxes each of six designs, and had similar results (1995). Professor Davis concluded that the sloping front of the Peterson box attracted the bluebirds (1995). But in 1996 and 1997, Professor Berner tested entrance hole designs, switching the Peterson and standard NABS entrance holes, and found that bluebirds selected the Peterson oval hole on a NABS box more often than on a Peterson box, while swallows chose the Peterson shape (1998).

The original Peterson design may seem too small for use by mountain bluebirds, but Alberta's mountain bluebirds have nested in them successfully. Enlarging the entrance hole to $1^1 2$" x $2^1/4$ "

could make the boxes more attractive to starlings.

In a two-year carefully -controlled Ellis Bird Farm (Alberta) study of 20 boxes of each style, mountain bluebirds showed no preference for any entrance hole or box style. (Pearman, 1999)

The western bluebird could use both the Peterson and the Gilbertson PVC box. Currently, the standard NABS nestbox is more often used for the western species.

Western bluebirders Pat Johnston and Brenda McGowan of Portland, Oregon, and long-time bluebirder Elsie Eltzroth of Corvallis, Oregon use a standard 5" x 5" (12.5cm x 12.5 cm) box with a $1^1/2$" (38mm) round hole [in areas where there is no overlap with mountain bluebirds]. Pat and Brenda and other volunteers have revitalized the well-known Hubert Prescott trails. They prefer 10 inch square roofs. Their boxes are 6"-7 " deep.

While many mountain bluebirders strongly advocate a box with at least a 5 x 5" floor and an entrance hole of $1^9/16$" (40 mm), Bob Wilson of Grand Junction, Colorado, has regularly fledged mountain bluebirds out of $1^1/2$" entrance holes.

In this chapter, we have given a brief overview of the more widely-used and recommended nest boxes. The appendix lists sources for plans, kits or finished boxes. There is no reason you cannot make your own box. There are, however, certain basics which make the difference between a " good" and a " bad" box: there must be adequate ventilation and insulation, and the entrance hole must fit a bluebird, not a starling. When opened, the box should allow clear observation and thorough cleaning. The box must never have a perch, which attracts house sparrows and wrens, and is not needed by any of the three bluebird species. Horizontal scratches below the entrance hole on the outside will provide toe hold for adult birds. Saw kerfsor scratches on the inside of boxes will aid fledging swallows but are not necessary for bluebirds.

49

There is friendly disagreement about the need for drain holes on the floor. Floors which have the corners cut off for extra ventilation may increase chances of eggs freezing or nestlings being chilled in extremely cold weather. However, if the box allows water to enter, and the nest remains wet, especially in cold weather, chicks may become hypothermic. Blowflies seem to be attracted to wet nests. Floor holes are not normally needed for ventilation, though it may seem helpful in drying out a wet nest or on a hot day if a cool breeze arises (and if the nest material does not block the holes!). Heat rises: ventilation holes toward the roof are what lets the heat escape. Perhaps floor vent holes are of more benefit in a deeper box (more than 6" from the bottom of the entrance hole to the floor).

Boxes with large overhanging roofs help keep moisture out and provide more shade over the sides and front of the box. The overhanging roof will also lessen the amount of moisture dripping off an adult bird entering the box during a rainy period. It should overhang the front at least $2^{1}/2$"; the more overhang, the less chance of predators reaching in from the top to grab the nest contents - eggs, nestlings, or incubating female. Slanting the roof forward enhances those features.

Dick Peterson did extensive research on temperature differences in thirteen different box styles. Boxes of styrofoam, boxes painted black, and boxes with a single 3/4" roof were 7°F hotter inside than the double-roofed Peterson when the outside temperature was 105°F. They also heated more quickly and cooled more slowly.

Zeleny (1976) found dark-colored boxes can be 12°F hotter than light-colored boxes. Since eggs and nestlings will literally cook to death above 107°F, we must strive for the lowest possible inside temperature.

There are adaptations which can further reduce the heat inside any nest box. If the permanent direction of the box is known, a a wide-overhanging roof can be mounted to one side so that the edge away from the afternoon sun is almost flush to that side, and the extra overhang is on the sunny side. An extra roof mounted an inch or so above the first roof (by spacers) also aids in reducing heat. Also, a false side can be added to that which receives most sun, with spacers between the two. One of the advantages of the Gilbertson system of mounting narrow conduit over rebar is not only that it is predator resistant if waxed, but the entrance of box and mount can be easily turned toward the early sun in spring, and turned away from the hottest sun of the day in summer. The idea is less easily applied to heavier supports. (See other hints for providing sun relief, Chapter 4.)

Slanting ventilation holes upward (toward the outside) may slightly aid ventilation, but should be done only if the roof widely overhangs the holes, sheltering them from rain. Boxes in the northern latitudes should have only small ventilation holes to reduce heat loss during inclement weather.

Sketches of the recommended boxes can be found at the end of this chapter. Plans for many of them are available from the North American Bluebird Society and various local bluebird organizations. (See Appendix for details.)

Most bluebirders have a strong preference for a particular type of nest box and are sure it is superior because the bluebirds return again and again to select the same box design, if not the very same box. Some people may believe there is very likely an imprinting or philopathic factor involved; that is, returning bluebirds who fledged the previous year tend to look for the same type of box from which they fledged. And second-year birds that nested successfully the previous year will use the same kind of box again. However, it is more likely that the habitat and the advantageous foraging is attractive and familiar to them.

So we emphasize again—if you are a beginning bluebirder, try several designs, within the basic overall recommendations. We all benefit by being open-minded, willing to experiment with new ideas even when we think we have the ideal box from which "our" bluebirds have the most success fledging their young with the least predation.

Remember: No design will take the place of frequent nestbox monitoring to insure that all is well on the bluebird trail!

The
Peterson
oval hole

Dick Peterson

Steve Gilbertson

Female eastern bluebird in Gilbertson PVC nestbox

PLATE   7

The Gilbertson
PVC nestbox

Steve Gilbertson

Svante Humbla

PLATE 8

Male
mountain
bluebird
near
St. Paul,
Minnesota

Terry Brashear

Tim Smalley

North American Bluebird Society nestbox

PLATE   9

Mountain
bluebirds
from Humane
 Society
fostered out
successfully.

Donna Hagerman

Boz Metzdorf

"You never listen to me!"

PLATE *10*

Peterson Nestbox

A. The Peterson box has seven parts and is assembled in this order:

B. The inner roof is toe-nailed to the back.

C. Then, the floor is toe-nailed to the back.

D. Third, one side is nailed to the resulting frame.

E. Then the other side is nailed to the frame.

F. Next the swing-down front is fastened by a nail into each side. A third nail is pounded part-way into the side near the entrance hole. This is removed each time the house is checked.

G. Finally, the outer roof is nailed on top.

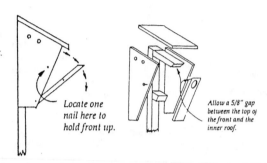

Locate one nail here to hold front up.

Allow a 5/8" gap between the top of the front and the inner roof.

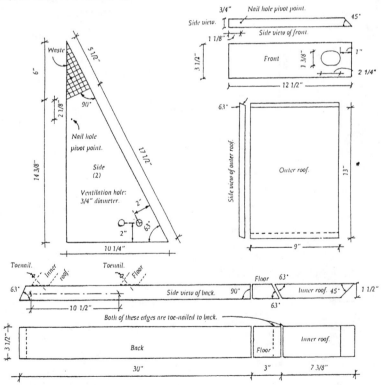

Gilbertson PVC Nestbox

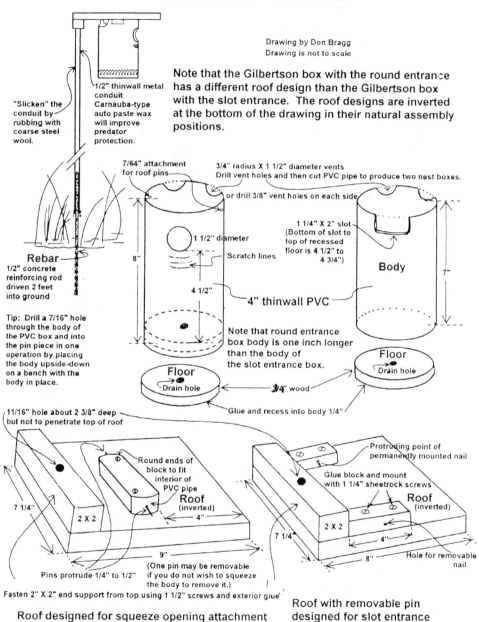

Drawing by Don Bragg
Drawing is not to scale

Note that the Gilbertson box with the round entrance has a different roof design than the Gilbertson box with the slot entrance. The roof designs are inverted at the bottom of the drawing in their natural assembly positions.

1/2" thinwall metal conduit

"Slicken" the conduit by rubbing with coarse steel wool.

Carnauba-type auto paste wax will improve predator protection.

7/64" attachment for roof pins

3/4" radius X 1 1/2" diameter vents
Drill vent holes and then cut PVC pipe to produce two nest boxes.

or drill 3/8" vent holes on each side

1 1/2" diameter

Scratch lines

1 1/4" X 2" slot
(Bottom of slot to top of recessed floor is 4 1/2" to 4 3/4")

Body

7"

Rebar
1/2" concrete reinforcing rod driven 2 feet into ground

8"

4 1/2"

4" thinwall PVC

Tip: Drill a 7/16" hole through the body of the PVC box and into the pin piece in one operation by placing the body upside-down on a bench with the body in place.

Note that round entrance box body is one inch longer than the body of the slot entrance box.

Floor
Drain hole

Floor
Drain hole

3/4" wood

Glue and recess into body 1/4"

11/16" hole about 2 3/8" deep but not to penetrate top of roof

Round ends of block to fit interior of PVC pipe

Protruding point of permanently mounted nail

Glue block and mount with 1 1/4" sheetrock screws

7 1/4"

2 X 2

Roof
(inverted)

4"

Roof
(inverted)

2 X 2

7 1/4"

4"

9"

(One pin may be removable if you do not wish to squeeze the body to remove it.)

8"

Hole for removable nail

Pins protrude 1/4" to 1/2"

Fasten 2" X 2" end support from top using 1 1/2" screws and exterior glue

Roof designed for squeeze opening attachment to round entrance PVC nest box

Roof with removable pin designed for slot entrance PVC nest box

54

Original NABS Nestbox

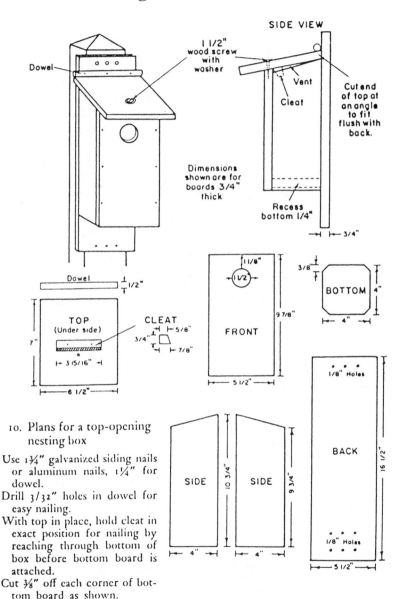

SIDE VIEW

Dowel

1 1/2" wood screw with washer

Vent

Cleat

Cut end of top at an angle to fit flush with back.

Dimensions shown are for boards 3/4" thick

Recess bottom 1/4"

3/4"

Dowel   1/2"

TOP (Under side)

7"

3 15/16"

6 1/2"

CLEAT

3/4"   5/8"

7/8"

11/8"

1 1/2

9 7/8"

FRONT

5 1/2"

3/8"

BOTTOM   4"

4"

1/8" Holes

BACK   16 1/2"

1/8" Holes

5 1/2"

SIDE   10 3/4"

SIDE   9 3/4"

4"   4"

10. Plans for a top-opening nesting box

Use 1¾" galvanized siding nails or aluminum nails, 1¼" for dowel.

Drill 3/32" holes in dowel for easy nailing.

With top in place, hold cleat in exact position for nailing by reaching through bottom of box before bottom board is attached.

Cut ⅜" off each corner of bottom board as shown.

Newer NABS Nestbox

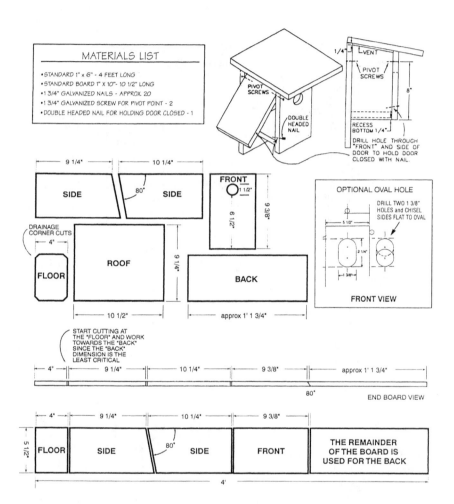

Troyer Slotbox

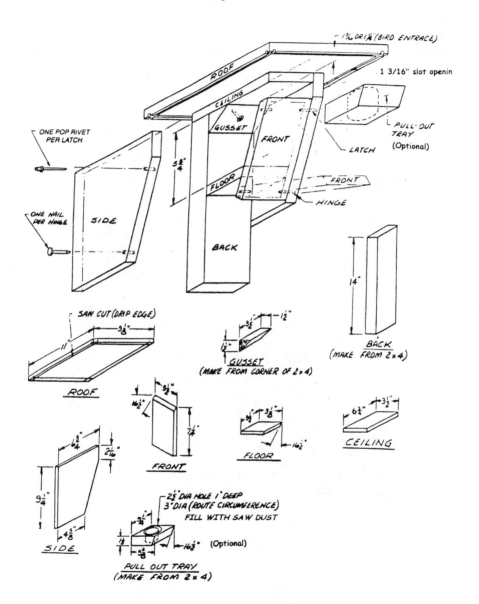

Notes

Chapter 4:

Creating a Bluebird Trail

The most beautifully crafted bluebird nest box meeting all the basic requirements is absolutely useless if it is not placed where bluebirds are likely to be attracted. It is actually detrimental if house sparrows or starlings are allowed to nest or if predation is not controlled.

Location

The term " bluebird trail" commonly refers to a group of five or more nestboxes placed for ease of monitoring. But those of you who have only a small space at your primary residence should not be deterred. There are two options for smaller areas. The first is: if there are no tree or violet-green swallows in the area, and you can take advantage of a block or break in the sight lines,(for instance a large building), put up one box on either side of the building. You could have bluebirds in both boxes. The second option is to put up two boxes fifteen to twenty-five feet apart (see Spacing and Pairing in this chapter). Bluebirds might occupy one, leaving the other for swallows. Initial attempts may be discouraging, but do not give up. Bluebirds are now increasing in number and reappearing not only in semi-urban areas, but in the middle of small towns and even close to large towns.   PVC boxes (see previous chapter) are especially recommended in urban areas where house sparrows are so abundant.

In Minneapolis, Mary McGee fought all the odds: flocks of house sparrows fed by a naive condominium dweller; a restricted space close to water; freight trains rumbling by seventy-five feet away; a frequently used Minneapolis park path; cats, raccoons, and vandalism. Within two miles of downtown skyscrapers, a pair of bluebirds arrived in late May of 1987 and again in 1988, successfully raising five fledglings the first year and three the second. In 1989 they nested three times, only to have eggs or young destroyed by wrens and vandals.

The bluebirds seemed to avoid nesting in 1991, but in 1992 there were five successful nests and 17 young fledged. Apparently warning signs on the nestboxes as well as in front of the boxes helped passersby keep the vandalism in check.

The second option, either as an alternative or following the first, is to go to where bluebirds are more likely to breed: along the edges of pastures, the outlying areas of farms, unsprayed golf courses and cemeteries, lightly traveled country roads, lesser used areas of county and state parks. Wide open areas with sparse or low ground cover with scattered trees, such as oak savanna, are ideal. The edges of agricultural areas with trees or perches nearby are excellent if pesticide spraying will not coincide with the nesting season.

Placement

Next to building or buying the proper nest box, placing and spacing in proper habitat is critical, much more so now than before the advent of house sparrows and starlings, and a more recently realized threat, house wren predation and usurpation.

Bluebirds need ground cover that is low or sparse, or both, for foraging. Areas that are stony and too infertile for more than sparse plant growth, such as gravel pits, serve well. Bluebirds will fly up to a mile for food if necessary, but the extra time and energy required impinges on their ability to keep the nestlings well and frequently fed. Open, sunny areas at least 200 feet from dense woods or brush, with a few scattered trees or saplings for perching,

60

are ideal. Wrens will probably cause trouble at shorter distances.

Other suitable sites are pastures, wide expanses of unsprayed lawn, golf courses, and cemeteries. Bluebirds will accept boxes in a much wider range of habitat, especially if there is a critical housing shortage. Proper placement will gain a much better chance of attracting them and will pose less threat to a successful nesting. There are usually diverse local conditions within a township, a county, or even on trails less than a mile apart. Be aware that the particular habitats and conditions on your trail can change. Be ready to move your boxes from year to year, always experimenting.

Bluebirds may surprise you by appearing in the least likely places, reflecting current needs and changing local predator conditions. The first thrill of the season, when a bluebird pair appears and goes in and out investigating several boxes, may turn to disappointment when they disappear for a few weeks. A break between arrival and serious nesting is common. Or that first pair sighted may really be on the way to the box they used last year. As the season progresses, a new younger pair may find their first nesting opportunity on your trail.

If one place seems ideal, but you are not having luck, continue to try it for a few years before giving up. If you attract chickadees, nuthatches, titmice, some tree swallows, or ashthroated or crested flycatchers (if the hole is too big), be grateful. Always make sure there are still empty boxes available. Bluebirds may nest even into late July, with some fledging in early September.

In the meanwhile, you may want to try a couple of boxes in a new location. Some of the best bluebird reports are from monitors whose trails lack most of the habitat " requirements." Don Mahle of Wabasha, Minnesota, has phenomenal success with boxes placed in wide areas so open there are no perching places or scattered trees, and quite far from water. In his case the mounted nestbox itself provided a perch for the adults. Fledglings who can, in their first attempt, fly only a hundred feet may end up fluttering in the grass before they reach cover and hop up to a branch. Good forage and lack of predation apparently outweigh the disadvantages of his open sites.

On the other hand, Judy Guninan found that the western bluebirds in her study area of Arizona preferred habitat less open than the large, open meadows preferred by eastern and mountain bluebirds, Open woods with small clearings, areas at the edges of fields, burned or logged areas and pine plantations attracted western bluebirds. Judy also felt the boxes in those areas should be spaced widely - at least 300 feet, because of territorial disputes between the pairs of western bluebirds.

Mountain bluebird territories in Alberta, Canada are two to three acres, but paired boxes (5'-15' apart) are used where tree swallow competition is high.

Those who have been bluebirding a long time are still changing, adding, and moving their boxes. A word of caution: do not increase your trails to the point that you cannot monitor them at least once a week. If they are not monitored or become a drudgery, remove them. This may seem harsh or unnecessary, but regular maintenance and cleaning are essential. If house sparrows or even the beneficial tree swallows completely take over a bluebird trail, you will ultimately be doing the bluebirds more harm than good.

Permission must always first be granted by the farmer, the property owner, the local utility company, or the manager of the cemetery, golf course, or park. Rarely are bluebirders refused once the advantages of attracting bluebirds are pointed out (see the Hjorts' letter in the appendix).

It is not wise to put up bluebird nest boxes unless you yourself can monitor them regularly. Many landowners, initially enthusiastic, find they have neither the time nor dedication that maintaining a good bluebird trail entails.

It's a delightful warm feeling when they do become involved, when a new bluebirder is "hooked." Plenty of good habitat remains, should you or they wish to expand or start another trail. **Caution:** Wherever you contemplate digging holes to accommodate mounting pipes or posts, first check with all your local utility companies to be sure there are no underground   lines - gas, electricity, telephone, or cable.   These are more likely to be alongside roads, but they could cross anywhere on your own private land. In Minnesota, there is one office, Gopher I, which will send out personnel to check all possible buried service lines along the proposed spots. This may apply to other states as well. You will be held liable for any line accident you may cause unless you get clearance. Tragedies some distance away have occurred as the result of pierced lines.

Spacing and Pairing

Spacing bluebird nest boxes at least 300 feet apart has been recommended for years because bluebirds are territorial. Not only will the male guard his territory, but the female is just as aggressive to other females. Many other species of birds are also territorial.

While we may be primarily bluebirders, we can also   accommodate and welcome most other native species, utilizing some ideas about spacing, pairing, and location of nestboxes.

When tree swallows or violet-green are absent (determined from the previous year, as they usually return later than bluebirds), the 300-foot or more spacing can be retained.   Swallows prefer water nearby, but they will travel some distance to nest. With more and more tree swallows using bluebird nest boxes, experiments were undertaken to ensure at least some boxes remained available for bluebirds.

Pairing proved to be the best answer: two boxes close together, with at least 300 feet or more to the next pair. Depending on the population pressures, distances between the each box of a pair sight can be from 10 to 30 feet. Boxes close to water may be paired closer together. Without sight lines to the next pair, the distance between pairs may be closer. This would occur, for instance, if someone's home or a stand of trees was between the two pairs In California, for western bluebirds, the recommendation of the California Bluebird Recovery Program is 10 to 12 feet between boxes of a pair, and about 90 yards between pairs. There, the boxes may be shared not only with violet-green or tree swallows, but the ash-throated flycatcher may take up a box after the first brood of bluebirds have fledged.

In Montana, people like Art Aylesworth and Bob Niebuhr usually have no need to pair boxes. Art recommends five nestbox locations per mile in open country for both mountain and western bluebirds, but where there is a swallow problem, along a river, for instance, he puts boxes no more than 10 feet apart. "I have had seven miles of paired boxes as above for fourteen years and it works very well."(1997).

Even if swallows are not present, the female bluebird may utilize the next box in the pair when the first brood has not fledged. The male parent may be still caring for them while the female moves over to lay eggs before the first brood fledges.

The very comprehensive " Analysis of the Interspecific Competition of Eastern Bluebirds, Treee Swallows, and House Wrens " [in Delaware] which Richard Tuttle wrote(1991) bears review by anyone wondering about pairing. He outlined the different peaks in egg laying of bluebirds and swallows, the evidence that tree swallows act as guardians against wrens to protect bluebirds, and concludes that tree swallows do not have a lasting negative effect on the reproduction of eastern bluebirds. " Since bluebirds nest twice and swallows once, [unpaired] boxes used first by bluebirds may not have been available for the second nesting since they were occupied by swallows. The solution to to this problem is simple: paired boxes should greet each new nesting season at sites where a solitary box produced both swallows and bluebirds during the previous year."

Kevin Berner, Chair of the Research Committee for the North American Bluebird Society wrote: "In areas with House Sparrows, box pairing may reduce the chances of sparrows destroying a bluebird nest. A sparrow may be more likely to kill established bluebirds (or swallows) at a single box than if an empty paired box exists nearby. If a sparrow begins a nest in an empty box, the monitor could remove the sparrow before it interferes with the nest of a native species.

" I believe that in areas of high Treee Swallow densities, close pairing of nestboxes with the pairs widely spacedis the best management strategy for bluebirds."(Berner, 1998)

In 1994 Steven G. Parren wrote: "Current recommendations of 20 to 25 foot pairing of boxes to manage bluebird-tree swallow competition and placement of boxes (or pairs of boxes) at 300 foot intervals to limit competition among nesting bluebirds seems appropriate. If nesting boxes are placed about 100 feet apart, Tree Swallows will have more nesting site choices than bluebirds." (Parren, 1994)

To sum up, the advantages of pairing are many:
(1) Both bluebirds and tree and violet-green swallows are territorial to a degree, but each will allow another species in its territory;
(2) Their feeding patterns differ (tree and violet-green swallows are aerial feeders, bluebirds are ground feeders), so there is not serious competition for food;
(3) It is much easier for a bluebird pair to defend its chosen box;
(4) Tree and violet-green swallows are superior acrobats, often helping to defend both boxes from predators, especially wrens and house sparrows.

Mounting Nestboxes

Height. Nestboxes should be erected so the monitor can see into the nest. This means a minimum of 5 feet from the ground. A few stalwart bluebirds employ bicycles, ATVs, four-wheelers, and even a ladder in the back of a pickup to check much higher boxes.

Direction. Bluebirds have nested in boxes with the entrance holes facing every direction of the compass. In Minnesota surveys, the nestboxes most often chosen by bluebirds faced, in order of preference: east, northeast, south and west. Prevailing winds, sightlines to a safe perch, direction away from auto traffic, and direction of the hottest sun should be considered. Local weather should also determine the direction of the hole (Tschida, 1989).Nest boxes can circle a large field, making it easy for the monitor to walk and to detect the triggering of sparrow traps across the field as the boxes are monitored.

Fenceposts. In the past, the easiest and cheapest way to erect single nestboxes was along fencelines at 300-foot intervals. A few nails and a hammer were the only requirements, and checking boxes along a straight line was convenient. As tree cavities disappeared, bluebirds nested wherever they could, even in rural mailboxes and stovepipes. Wooden fenceposts, excavated by woodpeckers or starting to rot, attracted them.

However, more often than not, fencelines turn into predator highways, providing easy access for raccoons, feral cats, snakes, squirrels, and mice. Rarely are fenceposts tall enough to mount boxes more than five feet from the ground. If separate posts are not an option, try at least to mount the box with an extension (conduit for instance) above the post and protect it from climbing predators.

Hanging Nest Box and Lifter

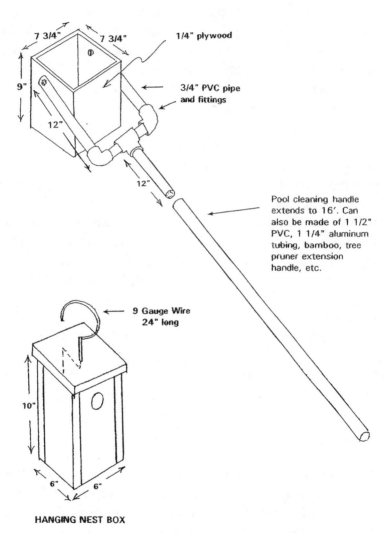

7 3/4"

7 3/4"

1/4" plywood

9"

3/4" PVC pipe
and fittings

12"

12"

Pool cleaning handle
extends to 16'. Can
also be made of 1 1/2"
PVC, 1 1/4" aluminum
tubing, bamboo, tree
pruner extension
handle, etc.

9 Gauge Wire
24" long

10"

6"   6"

HANGING NEST BOX

Dick Purvis Jan 1996

Sialia, Autumn 1997

Trees. Although bluebirds have nested successfully in tree-mounted nest boxes, which may seem a more natural site, keeping squirrels from chewing up the boxes, and climbing predators out is usually impossible when nestboxes are simply tacked onto the trunk an existing tree. The exception would be where there is a single strong tree in open habitat, and the trunk of the tree could be firmly wrapped with strong tin or metal.

While we would usually caution that nestboxes should never be put on trees, Dick Purvis of Annaheim California, has initiated a relatively safe method of hanging boxes high in large trees. He has fledged many bluebirds with this method. The idea has caught on in southern California. It has some advantages in special situations - pastures, public parks, vandalism-prone areas. The boxes are shaded from the hottest sun; by hanging them by hooks far out on sturdy limbs, there are beyond the daring of most raccoons. He is able to regularly monitor the boxes by employing a long rod and a box to carefully lift the boxes off a limb and down for observation. (Purvis, 1998)

Linda Violett of Yorba Linda, California follows this method, but after losing some boxes during a high wind, she shortened and doubled the hook portion. The only climbing invaders were black ants, which she stopped with some Tanglefoot® on the wire.

Separate Posts

Natural posts. As we back away from fenceposts and trees, mounting boxes may become more expensive. Small limbless dead trees and large straight limbs dug into the ground are hardly worth the trouble, rotting at ground level within a year or two. Wrapping them tightly with metal sheeting to eliminate paw holds is impossible, though cone guards can be placed just below the boxes.

Utility Poles. Utility poles along infrequently traveled roads are convenient and the overhead wires provide superb perching site. It is tempting to mount boxes on these thick posts which provide shade, and wrapping sheet metal below the box would deter predators. However, using such poles should never be done without authority from the telephone or power company. Without that permission, boxes may be destroyed by linemen at any time, and toxic chemicals may be heavily sprayed along the lines during peak nesting time. Most power companies have a safety policy to never allow attachments to power poles. They may remove and destroy boxes. There are times when they cannot use basket trucks. Even nails and screws prevent use of linemen's " hooks" and they may slip and fall.

Bluebirds are more likely to become traffic fatalities on high-traffic roads, even with the entrance hole facing away from the road. Kestrels also love telephone or power lines as perches (See Chapter 7 PREDATION). In states where mourning doves may be legally hunted, there is additional hazard—bluebirds have also been shot.

Commercial wooden posts. Either 4" x 4" square or $3^{1}/2$" diameter or larger round commercial posts (smaller ones are not sturdy enough), 6 ft. to 8 ft. long, can be set 2 ft. into the ground. Wooden posts which are green-colored probably have been treated with copper arsenate (see comments about copper arsenate in Chapter 3 - Nestboxes). Dirt should be mounted up around the base so that water will not accumulate there. Discount lumber stores often have special sales on treated posts. Commercial posts are smooth and can be wrapped tightly and smoothly with overlapping large sheets of metal starting at the bottom and extended to the bottom of the box.

Metal posts. Farmers' T-posts 6 ft. to $7^{1}/2$ - ft. long used for fencing have small knobs extending the entire length. These are the least expensive of purchased metal posts, and may even be available free from ex-dairy farmers, but the knobs can provide footholds for hungry raccoons. A long piece of PVC pipe slipped over the T-post under the box, and regularly greased will help prevent climbing. Boxes on T-posts must be mounted securely with wire or pipe strapping so that they don't slide around or down.

More expensive and more difficult to find are the commercial 6 ft. or 8 ft. highway sign posts commonly used in state parks. Of two types, one has holes the length of the post; the other, obviously safer, has the holes starting at about 4 $^1/2$ ft. up. The holes are one inch on center, which makes mounting with 3$^1/2$" carriage bolts and washers easy if the box is predrilled with holes 3" on center. State park managers may donate the poles for park bluebird trails. Try to select posts without rust or deep scratches.

Some park and cemetery managers have given permission to mount bluebird boxes directly on the backs of existing signs. Wind vibration doesn't seem to bother the bluebirds. The sign itself provides a perch above the box for feeding and guarding and may even act as a shield against blowing rain and snow. The box is also less visible to vandals. Extra predator guards will probably be necessary.

Pipe. Smooth clean pipe makes an ideal mounting post. An 8 ft. length can be driven 2 ft. into the ground. The Oschwalds, of Sumner, Texas, use 3/4" schedule 40 galvanized pipe. One-inch (nominal) water pipe is sturdy and not easily climbed by predators, especially if it is sanded smooth and waxed.

Smooth pipe can also be treated with a silicone spray used for automobiles. Silicon does not deteriorate, does not have to be reapplied frequently, nor does it collect debris the way grease does. One-half inch conduit pipe smoothed with steel wool and waxed with carnauba wax prevents most climbing, and is also long lasting.

Four easy and inexpensive methods of mounting are:
(1) If the pipe is threaded at the top and you are using a flat-bottomed nest box, it can be attached with a pipe flange.
(2) Any nest box can be attached through the back by predrilling the pipe and the back and using carriage bolts or lag screws.
(3) Three 5"pieces of pipe strapping and six screws can be employed. Fasten one piece vertically to the back of the house, bending the top half over to insert in the top of the pipe. Put the other two pieces across the pipe horizontally about 12" apart.
(4) The nest box can be attached with wire. But wire may break under stress of twisting and, unless both box and post are pre-drilled, it is impossible to attach the box to the pipe securely.

E.J. Schaefer (1992) of Sauk Rapids, MN suggests that $1^1/4$" pipe is available very reasonably from well-drillers, who are usually willing to cut it. All used pipe which cannot be made absolutely smooth can be made climb-proof by the addition of narrow PVC pipe extended over it at least two feet from below the nest box, or by 2" plastic downspout fitted over it. Also, check over-head garage door companies. They often have used smooth round pipe which can be easily cleaned.

Two sizes of galvanized thick-walled conduit, $1/2$" and $3/4$" inside diameter, erected concentrically, are suggested by Dew and Leighton (1986). Two 10-ft. lengths of pipe will provide posts for two boxes: each length is cut in half. The resulting 5 ft. section of 1/2" pipe is pounded 18—24 inches into the ground and the larger diameter pipe slipped over it. Rocks or pieces of wood will keep it from sinking more than a few inches into the ground. Steve Gilbertson (1990) uses 1/2" conduit over 1/2" rebar (concrete reinforcing bars) in a similar fashion. (Conduit is measured by inside diameter, rebar by outside diameter, so the conduit slips over the rebar.) For a heavier nestbox, use 3/4" material.

It is necessary to drill through the box into the larger pipe, or secure it very tightly with pipe clamps or strapping, to prevent the box from sliding around or down the pipe. If the nest box top overhangs the back by at least $^1/2$", that edge will keep the box from slipping down; alternatively, a nail through the pipe strap can secure the box. The larger pipe may turn on the smaller one, necessitating a bolt through both. With conduit, a conduit connector will work, with a shorter screw on top. Narrow pipes will sway in a high wind, but once the bluebirds have claimed the box, this does not seem to frighten them away. The mounting should be waxed for extra precaution against climbers.

PVC Pipe. An ideal but higher-priced mounting device, large smooth PVC pipe is fairly secure against climbing predators. It should be at least $1^1/2$" or 2" in diameter. It, too, should be waxed or greased or sprayed with silicone, The box can be attached with bolts or, if the pipe end is threaded, with a flange. The PVC pipe should go 2 feet into the ground, with the box mounted at least 5 feet above ground. (In the south, snakes have climbed 4-ft. PVC pipe.) Deep scratches on the pipe could yield toe-holds for predators.

Paul Chance, of Laurel, Delaware (1996) uses a telescoping. or elevator post arrangement. By using two sections of PVC pipe (one $1^1/2$" diameter and the other 2", and a 10-penny nail, he can raise

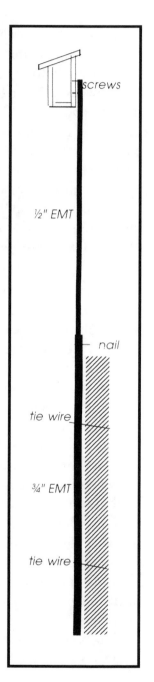

his nestboxes up to 7 feet. (Bluebirds have occupied boxes 15 feet (4.5m) or more above the ground.) Holes drilled for the nail through both sections (while extended) provides a locking mechanism. Removing the mail lowers the box for monitoring.

Chance's elevator pole idea has been modified slightly by Hatch Graham, of the California Bluebird Recovery Program, who suggests using electric metal tubing (EMT) or thin-wall pipe which is slightly less expensive than PVC. Materials include a 5-foot section of 1/2" EMT pipe, another $4^1/2$-foot section of 3/4" EMT, a 16 penny nail, two 1" deck screws to secure the nestbox through pre-drilled holes in the top of the EMT, and two 10" pieces of black tie wire or baling wire. A 3/8" hole is drilled through both pipe to provide the 16d nail locking device.

Climbing Guards

Cones. Wide metal cones or shields, installed under the nestbox can stop all climbing predators. These should be at least 24" in diameter and preferably 30", mounted five feet or more above the ground. Jack Jensen and Darwin Arndt of Madelia, Minnesota, found they could use grain deflectors out of corn storage bins to make these cones, and they were able to completely conquer their raccoon problems of previous years by use of the cones. Jaclyn Hill of Ellsworth, Iowa, has been very successful using plow disk blades. Sheet metal may be easier to find, but it should be fairly rigid. The inverted cone can be supported by pieces of strap iron or wood blocks or by tabs cut from the inner circle. The illustration of the 36" diameter cone is taken from Dr. Lawrence Zeleny's book (1978).

Aluminum Sheets Large (2-ft. x 3-ft.) sheets of used aluminum (sometimes called printer's tin) used to be available at small printing companies. It's necessarily a messy job handling them,

Jensen-Arndt Raccoon Guard

For large wood <u>posts</u>

Adjust center hole for different size posts.
7" center fits
$5\frac{1}{2}$ to $6\frac{1}{2}$ posts. ➞

For <u>boxes</u> on steel or small wood posts.

Bend 3 tabs up on bottom of
2 x 4 back of box. ➞

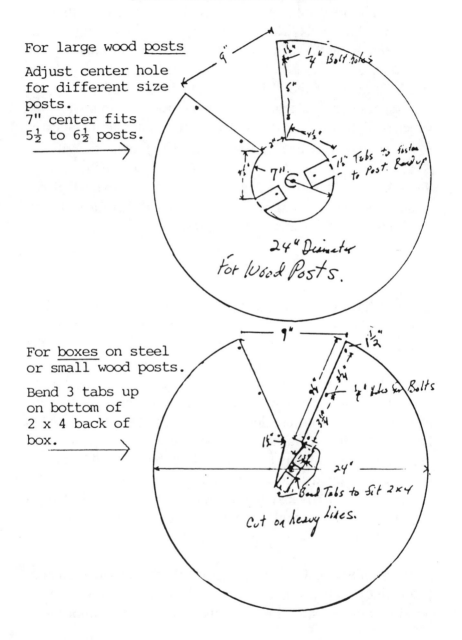

24" Diameter
For Wood Posts.

Cut on heavy lines.

Zeleny Raccoon Guard

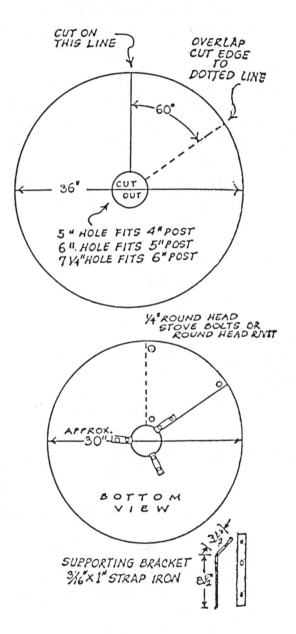

CUT ON THIS LINE

OVERLAP CUT EDGE TO DOTTED LINE

60°

36"

CUT OUT

5" HOLE FITS 4" POST
6". HOLE FITS 5" POST
7 ¼" HOLE FITS 6" POST

¼" ROUND HEAD STOVE BOLTS OR ROUND HEAD RIVIT

APPROX. 30"

BOTTOM VIEW

SUPPORTING BRACKET
³⁄₁₆" X 1" STRAP IRON

75

as they have printer's ink on one side. The sheet should extend at least three feet down below the box rather than from ground level up, which would allow cats to leap above it. (Cats have been known to leap up 62 inches to the top of a nestbox.) These used sheets are getting harder to find. New aluminum sheets are easier. **Grease**. Heavy automobile grease regularly applied over the entire length of wooden posts, or preferably metal posts, may discourage raccoons. Some people have added cayenne pepper to the grease as an added repellant. Ordinary chassis grease is heavy, difficult to apply, and dries out.

Wheel-bearing or lithium grease last longer, but all grease dries out and accumulates debris. According to Krueger (1989), a mixture of five pounds of chassis grease with one quart of turpentine will stay soft and keep the right consistency.

Wooden poles absorb the grease; metal posts and sheet aluminum do not. Jack Sprenger of Mankato, Minnesota, can attest to raccoon paw marks right through the fresh grease on his wooden posts and up to the hole. Thick grease can be a barrier to ants as well, if applied regularly. It also can be used on hanging hummingbird and oriole feeders. Steve Gilbertson, of Aitkin, Minnesota, has an idea for 'self-greased' pipes: with duct tape, attach small pint bags filled with grease around the pipe near the bottom of the box. Any creature with claws will pierce the bags when it reaches them!

The commercial product Tanglefoot®, available in garden stores, has the same undesirable traits as grease. It is less apt to contaminate the soil, but it is also possible to trap small beneficial insects and, in one case, a fledging songbird. It also collects wind-blown debris, as does grease.

PVC Pipe. Four-foot lengths of hard PVC over pipes may stop climbers, especially if it is sprayed with silicone, or rubbed wax or lithium or wheel-bearing grease. Squirrels have eventually been able to scratch their way up a non-treated 3" PVC pipe under a feeder , and raccoons may to be able to do likewise.

Stovepipe. Many people find that lengths of stovepipe hanging or fastened underneath a nestbox over the pipe or post make good "stoppers" against climbing predators. It does have a tendency to get scratched or dented.

Downspout. Rectangular aluminum downspout is inexpensive, works especially well and is difficult for snakes to climb. Coat hanger wire can be used to attach it underneath the box. Allen Bower, of Britton, Michigan, uses a 30" piece of either brown aluminum downspout or 4" PVC stained brown, and, as an extra precaution to anything climbing inside them, caps them off at the top with a plastic bottle. His mounting poles are 3/4" pipe. The plastic bottle should have a snug fit around the top of the guard, as a snake can squeeze through even a 1/2" opening, and a mouse can squeeze through anything it's head can fit in. The guards and bottles are slipped over the post before the nestbox is attached. First drill holes for the wire 1" from the top of either the downspout or PVC guard; slip the guard over the post, slip the bottle over the guard temporarily to measure an inch clearance under the box, mark the pole where the wire will go through it from the guard, and then drill through the post for the wire, and insert the wire through

the outside of the guard, through the post and through the other side of the guard. Bend the wire down about 30° and back up over the top of the guard. For the downspout cap, Allen uses a 32-oz. vinegar bottle; for the 4" PVC a 2-liter pop bottle. Obviously the size of the bottles and their necks have to be adapted to the mounting post diameter. Leaving some of the bottom of the bottles will make a snug fit. (Bower, 1999)

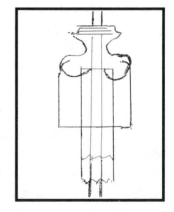

Predator Guards

Just as quickly as one bluebirder claims to have an absolutely unclimbable post, another bluebirder proves the claim wrong! And as soon as we are sure we have no predators in the area, the next year changes the picture. There is no avian predator worse than the house sparrow, which we can only trap rather than guard against (see Chapter 7: PREDATORS), but climbing predators can be stopped using predator guards as well as tall, smooth posts.

All trails are different in predator potential. Even on the same trail, weather and hunger (and mouths to feed) will determine how hard a specific predator tries. Experiment with some of the following predator guards, which may be installed on, in, or below the nest boxes.

Wooden hole guards
Some bluebirders like a thick wood block, usually a piece of 2' x 4', (which is actually $1^1/2$" thick) over the nest box entrance, with a corresponding hole in its center. Presumably a mammalian predator has difficulty reaching in and bending its paw down through the extra thickness. It might also help keep rain out of the box, but bluebirds will usually avoid a box with a total entrance hole thickness of more than $1^1/2$" if a thinner entrance is available. The North American Bluebird Society no longer recommends the predator blocks.

Wire hole guards.
Jim Noel, of Ashland, Illinois, devised a $3^1/2$" x $5^1/2$" wire mesh box which fits over the entrance hole, its sides stapled to the edge of the door. The door edges usually have to be shaved to accommodate the extra thickness of the wire mesh. With Jim Noel's approval, John Thompson, of Rochester, Minnesota, fashioned an

Noel Guard With Adapter

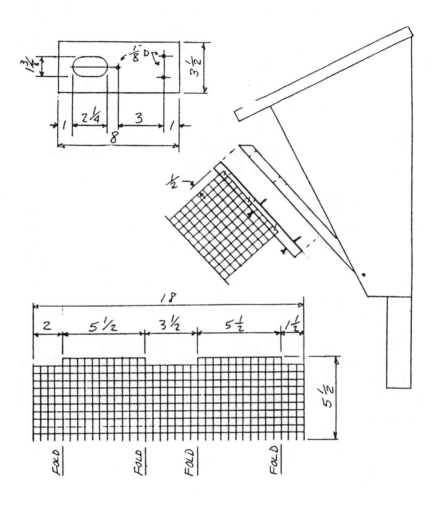

adapter. The wire guard is preattached to a large block of wood which has a matching entrance hole, and the guard with adapter is attached with three screws. The guard to be easily transferred to another box.

Field tests with the Noel guard have been very successful. Initially attached after the first egg was laid, bluebirds may also begin nesting with it in place, especially if they are familiar with it from an earlier nesting.. Be sure to use a heavy, welded or soldered $1/2$" wire mesh. The "seam of the mesh should be on the top, so there is no chance of a bird's foot being caught in it. Use heavy stapling. Raccoons, especially, are very strong.

Plastic hole guards. There are several plastic hole guards on the market, ranging from dark brown, to translucent, to one with holes. Another one has a tail brace to make it more acceptable. The chances of bluebirds using them are slim. They should be attached only after the first egg is laid, and then the nestbox carefully watched to be sure the female will eventually go in.

The last three predator guards do not allow the adult bluebirds to feed the young by clinging to the outside of the box and extending food to the young; adults actually must enter the box, feed the young, then turn around to exit. Obviously the extra work may be preferable to losing the eggs or nestlings.

Extra Options

Extra enticements and precautions are worth trying. Ingenuity knows no bounds among bluebirders!

Water
Bluebirds love to bathe, and of course they need water. If you are fortunate enough to have bluebirds in or near the yard, a birdbath

adds to the attraction. Lawn sprinklers will attract them also, but incidentally - not something they can regularly find.

Bathing tends to cool the birds and helps remove any external parasites before preening. It's a social activity for them. Bird bath water should be kept fresh and clean. A concrete bath provides a rough bottom for good footing. Depth should be not more than two inches. If a birdbath heater is installed in baths in winter, the cost will be only a few pennies a day to run and the bath will be enjoyed by other, non-migrating birds.

Eating snow lowers birds' metabolic rate, especially in extreme cold.

Perches

Bluebirds will use convenient perches that are well off the ground and within fifty feet or so of the nest box to scan for food and to guard the box. Dave Curtis and Shelly Smith of Wyoming, Minnesota, found their bluebirds love to perch on the cross bars of nearby radio towers. In wide open fields, with no cover, trees, or wires nearby, a tall perch (a stake or small dead tree five feet or more high) can be stuck in the ground.

Svante Humbla, of Cincinnati, OH, uses tall perches of 1/2" electrical conduit with a 3/8-inch wood or PVC crossbar near the top, and has found that, placed at strategic points leading to woods, enables bluebirds to utilize boxes several hundred feet from shelter. It will also serve as a temporary landing perch for fledglings. Robins, flycatchers, and swallows will also benefit from such perches.

Steve Eno of Raymond, Nebraska utilizes a small diameter white fiberglass rods used for electric fences. A 14" cross bar is situated about 3 inches above the top of a 4-foot section. The short, small perches can be easily moved around.

Artificial shade

Bluebird eggs are normally incubated at 93°—100°F. Bluebird nestlings can tolerate, but only for a short time, 107°F in the nest box. In an unusual and prolonged hot period, artificial shade should be considered. Here typical bluebirder ingenuity really shines!

Consider these ideas for starters: a large piece of plywood, a fresh branch with leaves, an old umbrella, even a makeshift sail can be tacked on an extension above the box; an extra roof may be put over the existing one, with a wide overhang on the sunny side; an extra side with a spacer will help cool the hot side; even sticking a leafy branch into one of the vent holes or between the post and the box may help. People have put aluminum foil on the roof to reflect the heat (in which case you may want to be sure there is something else close by on which they can land before entering the nestbox, like the second box of a pair, or a sapling. In an area of tall trees widely spaced out in the open, nestboxes can be placed to take advantage of the afternoon shade of a tree.

Warmth

In late winter or early spring, when there is still danger of extreme cold or freezing rain, returning bluebirds will appreciate a tight box. (Small bare branches wedged horizontally inside during winter will provide roosting perches for wintering birds.) Small pieces of insulating strips pushed into the vent holes will make the boxes more snug until warm weather is ensured. The extra tightness of the box may make a critical difference to early incubating and brooding females, to eggs, and to nestlings. (Be sure to unplug the holes before hot weather sets in!). A simple floor-size piece of cardboard or smooth rigid material can be slipped under an early nest, to close over any existing drainholes, and slipped out later.

82

Keith Radel of Faribault, Minnesota, turns his Gilbertson boxes (mounted on conduit over rebar) toward the sun just for early spring. The usual seasonal wind direction should also be taken into account..

Svante Humbla, of Cincinnati, Ohio, has created sets of custom shutters for Peterson, Gilbertson and standard nestboxes. They can be permanently attached, even as the box is being constructed, and easily raised and lowered in accordance with current weather conditions.

The shutter for the Gilbertson box is a $2^1/2$" (64mm) wide, $5^1/2$" (144mm) long piece of the same 4" PVC as the box. A $^3/16$" -L-shaped slot with the right end slightly lower is cut in this piece, and secured with a screw, washer and nut. (As the shutter is turned to the left, it will move slightly forward to make a tight contact with the roof.) By loosening the nut the shutter can be dropped down to clear the vent voles. The shutters for the Peterson and standard boxes are made of $^1/4$" lattice, lath, any wood. They are also secured with scews and washers, with the corners rounded so they don't interfere with the roof as they swing open for ventilation.

Svante Humbla's Shutters

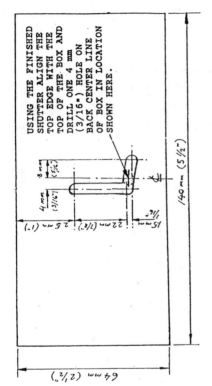

USING THE FINISHED SHUTTER ALIGN THE TOP EDGE WITH THE TOP OF THE BOX AND DRILL ONE 4 mm (3/16") HOLE ON BACK CENTER LINE OF BOX IN LOCATION SHOWN HERE.

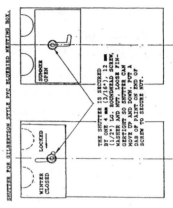

SHUTTER FOR GILBERTSON STYLE PVC BLUEBIRD NESTING BOX

SUMMER OPEN

LOCKED

WINTER CLOSED

THE SHUTTER IS SECURED BY ONE 4 mm (3/16"), 12 mm (1/2") LG. ROUNDHEAD SCREW, WASHER AND NUT. LOOSE FIN-GERTIGHT SO SHUTTER CAN MOVE UP AND DOWN. PUT A DAB OF PAINT ON END OF SCREW TO SECURE NUT.

Shutter for Gilbertson Box

is made of 4" thin-wall PVC pipe, as is the box itself. Cut a 2 1/2" (64mm) wide by 5 1/2" (144mm) long. Make a template of thin cardboard or paper. Bend it over the piece of PVC and trace outline and slot. Drill three 3/16" (4mm) holes at the ends & corner of the slot, and cut out lines with a coping saw. (Note: right end of L slot is slightly lower than the vertical part. In turning the shutter to the left it will move slightly forward to contact the roof tightly, as it locks into place.) Mark screw hole on box body by removing roof and sliding shutter up on back of box, with top edges flush and shutter center line lined up with back center of box. (Rubber bands will hold it in place). Drill 3/16" (4mm) hole just to the right of the bend in the L, as shown. Insert screw from inside box, with washer and nut on outside of shutter. When cold season starts, just raise shutter and twist to lock.

84

Svante Humbla's Shutters

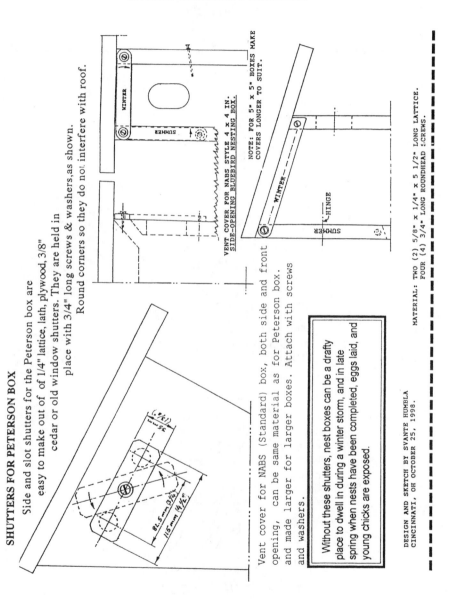

SHUTTERS FOR PETERSON BOX

Side and slot shutters for the Peterson box are easy to make out of 1/4" lattice, lath, plywood, 3/8" cedar or old window shutters. They are held in place with 3/4" long screws & washers, as shown. Round corners so they do not interfere with roof.

Vent cover for NABS (Standard) box, both side and front opening, can be same material as for Peterson box, and made larger for larger boxes. Attach with screws and washers.

Without these shutters, nest boxes can be a drafty place to dwell in during a winter storm, and in late spring when nests have been completed, eggs laid, and young chicks are exposed.

NOTE: FOR 5" x 5" BOXES MAKE COVERS LONGER TO SUIT.

VENT COVER FOR NABS STYLE 4 x 4 IN. SIDE-OPENING BLUEBIRD NESTING BOX.

MATERIAL: TWO (2) 5/8" x 1/4" x 5 1/2" LONG LATTICE. FOUR (4) 3/4" LONG ROUNDHEAD SCREWS.

DESIGN AND SKETCH BY SVANTE HUMBLA CINCINNATI, OH OCTOBER 25, 1998.

85

Notes

Chapter 5

Monitoring

Placing a beautifully crafted bluebird nestbox in an ideal location and mounting it well still does not transform one into a bluebirder. The third and final, and perhaps most important, essential ingredient is regular monitoring — checking the boxes at least once a week, early March through August, recording observations, and making necessary changes. Lucky are those who have bluebirds nesting in their back yards and can make daily observations. A great deal more effort and dedication is required if your trail is far from home and difficult to get to. Don't, in your initial enthusiasm, start with so many nest boxes that exhaustion soon replaces enjoyment. Put up a trail that you, as well as the bluebirds, will benefit from, one that will not be a burden on your time and energy.

When you put up even a single nestbox, you are making a commitment to help increase the bluebird population. It's not a "one-night stand" (not just a single six-week responsibility covering one nesting). Even in the rare circumstance of no resident house sparrows, no climbing predators, and no tree swallows, your fledgling numbers can be increased by regular monitoring. Without checking, there is no way to know for certain whether the house has been vandalized or occupied by bluebirds, when the eggs were laid, if the nestlings are all right, or have fledged, or if there are parasite or predator problems. And, if you know when to expect fledging, the box can be cleaned at the proper time and ready for a new nesting.

87

Furthermore, besides providing housing and helping the birds, the joy of bluebirding is in watching them develop and fledge successfully. Few wild birds will so readily accept human help and allow such close continuous observation. Beyond the self-satisfaction that comes from regular monitoring and record-keeping, sharing your observations adds to every bluebirder's knowledge— and there is so much yet to learn!

Checking

Monitor nest boxes at least once a week. Desertion of the nest after construction or abandoning the eggs because of disturbance is rare, but is more likely to occur before the eggs hatch. Do not believe the old wive's tale about songbirds abandoning because of human smell. Nests are sometimes deserted, but it is not because you have touched the nest, eggs or young. Although attachment to the clutch is strong after the first egg is laid, sometimes a female will desert her eggs during incubation if she is frequently disturbed or badly frightened.

Choose warm days, rather than cold, wet or windy ones, if you can. In the early nesting periods, when cold weather conditions persist, it is important that she stay on the eggs or return immediately. Always leave the box area quickly.

Some female bluebirds will remain on the eggs during inspection, even allowing themselves to be lifted up while the eggs are counted, and will stay there after the box is closed. Still others may become very agitated and "dive-bomb" the monitor, but will eventually return. Therefore it is better during the first few weekly checks to make some soft noises as you approach the box, to give the female time to fly out and perch nearby. If the male is near, he may warn her off, and may dive-bomb as well. Watch the box as you draw near. Tapping gently on the box before opening it will ensure that either she has left during your approach or that she will likely stay calm inside.

Thereafter, checking---even daily checking---done quickly,quietly, and carefully, will not disturb your bluebirds. The parents may dart from the nest box when they detect your presence or when you tap gently on the box, but they easily get used to your visits, and return more quickly each time. With the relatively short duration of each nesting cycle, it's obvious why weekly checking, at the least, is essential if accurate records are to be kept and boxes are to be readied for subsequent nestings. With frequent checking you will be better able to detect serious trouble and potential disaster. As Bryan Schantz says in his excellent small monograph, *Mountain BluebirdManagement* (1986): " Some people with a large [mountain bluebird] trails monitor their nestboxes only two or three times a season. While this is sufficient to determine what species is nesting and to clean out the nestboxes, it seldom is possible to help solve problems that might arise."

The nesting sequence detailed in Chapter 2: *Natural History* describes what you can expect to find. A nest is normally started and completed in one to six days, the second nest usually being built very quickly. One egg is laid each day, usually by mid-morning. Incubation begins as soon as the last egg is laid, though occasionally it may not commence for a few days. The incubation period before hatching is twelve to fourteen days. Depending on weather, nestlings are usually brooded during their first six days. Both parents will continue feeding the nestlings until they fledge —somewhere between the eighteenth and twenty-second day, earlier if the nest box becomes very warm or they are frightened into fledging prematurely, later if there is a cold snap.

Donald S. Pease documented in an amateur video the activities inside the nest, from egg-laying to fledging, (1998).

The Monitor's Pack

We all have our favorite method of carrying our 'tools of the trade' — our monitoring implements. A large, three-pocket carpenter's apron works well for some, a backpack or fanny pack for others.

Careful Monitoring Increases Occupancy

CAREFUL MONITORING OF
HOUSES INCREASES
OCCUPANCY

Linda
Peterson
Janilla

It may depend on what you use for record keeping (a big clipboard or a pocket-size notebook?) and also how far you have to be from bicycle, car, truck, ATV or home where you may keep a shovel, a big hammer, battery-charged drill or screwdriver, extra roofs or box fronts, used clean nests, a supply of mealworms, maybe even a small stepladder. Minimum requisites would probably include pliers, regular and Phillips screwdriver, a little brush, small plastic bags, a small box or towel to hold nestlings while replacing a wet nest, extra nails or screws (for when you drop the essential closing pin in tall grass!), your records, several pens or pencils, a small magnifying glass (to read that band when you gently open a box to discover a banded female still on the eggs). Short people with tall boxes may carry a small telescoping mirror and/or tiny gooseneck flashlight. A piece of cardboard or sturdy screen (see next section). Binoculars are a must with some of us. Tick or mosquito repellent. At the beginning of each season, a magic marker or whatever you use to renumber your boxes. Only experience will get you to the point where you complete a monitoring trip without forgetting *something*!

Moving or Lowering the Nest

The placement and mounting of bluebird nest boxes along a trail may vary. Despite our best intentions, we may leave boxes up that are not ideally situated or are open to predation. An "experienced" bluebird pair usually chooses wisely, but beginners — first-time nesters — may make the worst possible choice of boxes. The whole nest, once the eggs are laid and the nestlings hatch, can be moved, but with caution. It may be more difficult to actually move the whole box (in short graduated steps over a couple of days if the distance is long) to a safer mounting and re-attach it.

It is easier to set up a new nestbox and have it ready prior to the move. The entrance hole should face in the same direction and be at the same height (unless it is dangerously low). A piece of cardboard folded into a box of the same dimensions as the interior of the nestbox, but without top or back side, is easy to slip under the nest. The orientation of the nest should be the same as it was.

Frequently in the spring we find a nest that has been built up too close to the entrance hole. Or a second nest may be built on top of an old one. Even if cat or raccoon predation is not anticipated, the trail monitor should routinely lower a high nest after the first

91

egg appears. Slip a piece of cardboard, or your fingers under the nest, about three inches from the top of the cup, and remove the part below.

Read (1988) offers some cautions in lowering a nest: "When the nest contains only eggs, it is important not to change the orientation of the nest to the nest hole. If the nest contains young, it is not as important. It is, however, very important when young are less than nine days old to leave the cup area intact and make sure that a good inch of nesting material is left below it...."

When young are less than seven or eight days of age, the female broods them at night. If the nest is flattened out, the young may sprawl all over the bottom and the female cannot brood properly. A nestling that falls to one side of the box will not be retrieved. Obviously, the same precaution should be taken when the nest contains eggs. Read also cautions: " Do not attempt to lower a nest in a top-opening box unless the young are eight or nine days old and no cold weather is forecast for the next three days."

Safety first could be the motto of Jack Finch of North Carolina. In each of his nestboxes he inserts a cut-down peat (or pressed cardboard or spaghum moss) little starter pot, which just fits into his standard box. The mini-pot and its contents slip in and out easily for inspection. A custom-made box, of plastic or wire mesh, with a low front side, can be used as a tray in a similar fashion. This would be especially helpful in a second or third nesting, when the nest material may be sparse and the nestlings might fall out during inspection. Your notes should remind you about a flimsy nest, but always open a side or front door of a nestbox with care. Jean Romaner carries a thin piece of plexiglass, a little wider than the door opening, to slip across the box as the door is opened. It gives a clear view while the contents remain inside.

Jack Finch's peat pot nestbox 'tray'

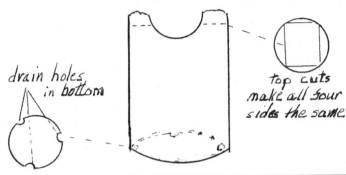

drain holes, in bottom

top cuts make all four sides the same

Eggs

Eggs, though warm when laid, will soon be cold to the touch until the female starts incubating. Normally this is when the clutch is complete, though she may delay a day or two after the last egg is laid. We may believe incubation of the eggs has started when actually it has not. The female may fly out of the box as we approach, and her four or five eggs appear to be warm. The eggs could be momentarily warm from her body as she laid the last egg.

If incubation has not started, bluebird eggs may be viable from at least a week to perhaps a month after they are laid, providing they are kept at temperatures between 50°F and 65°F. Occasional cooling during incubation does occur, and seems to cause no harm other than perhaps slowing development of the embryo. B.C. Pinkowski observed a bluebird nest in Michigan in which the first of six eggs did not hatch until the twentieth day of incubation. During that period the weather was unusually cold, often below freezing, and the female was not very diligent. Yet all six eggs eventually hatched!

On the other hand, the female may sense that the eggs are infertile, She may go elsewhere to start a new clutch, or occasionally, a new nest will be built over the first with its infertile or addled eggs, and a new clutch will be laid, either by the same female or

93

new one.

After incubation has actually begun, eggs may remain viable up to a day if the incubation is interrupted during the first week, but during the second week of incubation they will remain viable for only a few hours. This should be remembered if the female is found dead and there is a possibility of distributing the eggs to other bluebird nests where eggs are of the same age.

In transferring either unincubated or incubated eggs upon certain death of the female, be careful not to overload other nests. Gently mark with a soft pencil the transferred eggs as you do this, so that they can later be removed if they prove infertile or no longer viable. Examine the eggs carefully for tiny pinholes (indicating wrens may have been at work). Don't transfer any undersized eggs--they are not fertile. Eggs that appear half light and half grey are probably addled.

If no other bluebird nests on your trail are at a corresponding stage and no other bluebirder is nearby to contact, try using tree swallows nests, again being careful not to overburden them. Tree swallows have accepted bluebird eggs and successfully hatched and raised the nestlings along with their own. (It also has worked with house sparrows--they feed their young nestlings soft insects---but you shouldn't have any sparrows on your trail!) No studies have been done on the subsequent survival and communication these adopted birds have with their own species. We can only wish these "ugly duckings" have no relationship problems.

The above are just precautionary suggestions in case of trouble. Normally, all with go well, and the monitor can expect hatching to take place in about two weeks, or at least between 13 and 16 days after the last egg is laid. Some very hot days can start eggs incubating before the female herself starts the process, but only one or two eggs will be affected.

If one egg remains unhatched for some time in a clutch of nestlings, and the parents have not removed it, the monitor should probably take it out. It can break and soil the nest, and perhaps contaminate the live chicks with bacteria, though often it remains intact when the nestlings have fledged.

Nestlings

Parent bluebirds will rarely, if ever, abandon their nestlings. Even if one parent dies, the other can usually raise the young. The father can not incubate or brood the nestlings during their critical first five or six days. Zeleny (1988) provides some clues to nestling behavior which can help the monitor decide whether the nestlings are being cared for, even if there seems to be no parent around:

" An inexperienced observer on opening a nesting box may often be apprehensive on seeing that the nestlings appear completely limp and unresponsive. Nestlings more than about three days old usually react to human intrusion by crouching low in the nest and remaining almost completely motionless. Younger nestlings sometimes respond by stretching their necks upward uncertainly and opening their mouths to be fed. These are normal reactions to human intrusion and are in no way indicative of any kind of trouble.

``On rare occasions, older nestlings will respond to the opening of their nesting box by begging vigorously for food, and, if these baby birds are more than eight or nine days old, their begging may be very vocal. This reaction means that the birds are very hungry and have not been fed for some time. They may be abandoned, but perhaps the parent birds have just not supplied food at the usual time..."

While food is usually brought to the box every five or six minutes, the time may vary considerably, an hour or more passing before a parent returns. The nestlings can live up to twenty-four hours without food, but will be severely weakened by then. Remaining nearby to observe the box for several hours may be impractical. Instead, as suggested earlier, place something light across the entrance hole---some spider webs, a piece of thread, a tiny stick, a leaf, a piece of paper---something that the wind will not dislodge but that will be pushed out by a feeding parent. If a few hours later your suspicions are confirmed, it is time to distribute the nestlings to other nests, being careful to match the nestlings' ages and not overload the foster nests. (If both parents are providing food, eastern bluebirds can take care of six young. Schantz (1986) says "...if necessary, up to eight can be raised in a single [mountain bluebird] nest."

Note: Technically, you are breaking both state and federal laws by manipulating eggs or nestlings of protected migratory birds without a permit. Most local conservation officers (whom you should get to know) would be tolerant of such procedures on your own trail if you are an experienced bluebirder. They would be less happy if you are transporting eggs, nest, or fledglings some distance to another trail. Always check with your conservation officer.

Only under the most extreme conditions should a nestling be taken in an attempt at hand-raising. The only exception to the fostering process is when the nestlings are too weak to beg for food. If they cannot raise their heads up with beaks open, they will not be fed in a foster nest.

If delay in getting them to a licensed rehabilitator is unavoidable, keep them warm, gently force well-mashed mealworms, canned dog food, baby food, deep back into their throats. Moistening the food with Gatorade® may help, but do not force water alone. Very young nestlings rarely survive. Those about to fledge, or those left in the nest for some time after their siblings fledge, may survive (see Chapter 8). In either case, a special state and federal permit is needed to care for them. (And if you don't already have one, there won't be time!)

Nestlings that die after the first six or seven days of life are too heavy for the adults to remove, (The deeper the box, the more difficult the maneuver.) Any dead chick within a live brood should be removed immediately, of course, regardless of its age. The putrefaction of the carcass will soil the nest and will attract blowflies, carrion beetles, and predators. If the nest is already soiled in this manner, a new dry nest should replace it.

The late Earl Gillis studied daily temperature and weather patterns and their relationship to western bluebird survival for 14 years, near Newburg, Oregon (in the northern Willamette Valley). Below an average daily temperature of 52°F, intensified by wet or stormy weather, the chances of survival of nestlings aged 1-12 days was very poor. The majority of insects have been forced into hiding, and the female as well as the male will be away for too long trying to forage for food. Here again, supplementary food offered to parents can influence those chances.

Banding of nestlings, by those with proper banding permits, should be done between seven and thirteen days of age, after their legs are large enough, but before there is danger of causing premature fledging.

When Not to Check

Though top-opening boxes will allow observation of nestlings for a longer period, once the nestlings reach fourteen days old (see picture), they are alert to the outside world. They are then able to flutter, and they can be frightened by the front or the side of the box being opened and may panic and "eject." It is especially likely to happen if a watching parent sounds the alarm call. This, then, is one period when the box *should not be opened,* but rather observed at a distance.

Once the nestlings have fledged prematurely, there is little you can do; they will neither return to the box nor stay in it should you be lucky enough to locate all the half-fluttering, half-running young and get them all back in at once. The only reason to open the nest box at this time is if you, having observed the box from a distance, are quite sure something is wrong. For example, neither parent has appeared at the box for over two hours or there is evidence of predation on or around the box.

A hole reducer or some kind of constrictor may be employed if it is absolutely necessary to open the nest box. A hole-reducer is either (1) a thin block of wood with an even smaller center hole, large enough to allow food to be offered by parents, but too small to allow nestling (or parent) to pass through. It can be tacked over the entrance hole of nest boxes which do not have exterior predator guards. This should be left on for only a day or two. In no case should this be left on after the nestlings are sixteen days old. (2) Another kind of hole reducer, designed by Dick Peterson, employs the substitution of a new front in which there is a spring steel wire inserted at right angles into the wood below the hole and extended across the hole. The top of the wire, bent at 45°, fits into one of three grooves indented into the wood above the hole. By simply slipping a finger into the hole from the outside, the wire can be set in one of three positions. The first position effectively closes the entrance hole; the middle position will keep the young from pre-fledging, yet allows the parents to feed; and the thrid position leaves the hole wide open. A long fish line can be attached to the top of the wire and operated at some distance away.

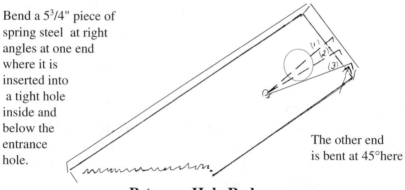

Bend a 5³/4" piece of spring steel at right angles at one end where it is inserted into a tight hole inside and below the entrance hole.

The other end is bent at 45°here

Peterson Hole Reducer

Keep in mind these blocks will prevent the removal of fecal sacs, and the nest will no longer be clean.

If the box is opened and quickly closed again with the birds making minimal attempts to fledge, and if the parents are not calling the young, you can place a simple obstruction (a rag, paper towel, piece of cardboard, or twig) across the hole. Then retreat to some distance. When fluttering in the box has ceased, quietly slip up and remove the obstruction.

The box should be watched frequently again for a matter of hours, if possible, for the parents' return. It's better to leave the nestlings even up to twenty-four hours than to remove them before you are sure the parents are gone.

Fostering them out at this age to other bluebird parents will probably only cause other premature fledging problems. Again, a special permit is required to keep nestling bluebirds to try to raise by yourself.

Donna Hagerman, an experienced Nevada researcher and western and mountain bluebirder, was successful against the odds:

" Last July [1998] I had a call from our local Humane Society saying that they had two mountain bluebirds which they had raised by hand for the last several weeks. Now they wanted to let them go, but were concerned that the birds didn't know how to hunt. So I went down there to find these two young birds well past the fledging age, at least a month old. They were flying very well... they weren't tame however.

" My only thought was to add them to a box of young who were just about ready to fledge, and use a hole constrictor so they would stay inside for a few days ... long enough to get the hang of being bluebirds and bond with the new family. I was lucky to find a family of six young just about 17 or 18 days old. I was really hoping to find a family of four or less, but beggars can't be choosers. So I developed this box with a big slot sectioned off with nails rather than a hole. With this design, more young would have a

99

shot at the food, especially since there would be eight inside and unable to get out. I mounted a tub of mealworms on a nearby branch. Those parents thought they had died and gone to bluebird heaven! This box was about 25 miles out of town but I drove out daily to replenish the mealworm supply and check on them. On the third day, I removed one nail and sat back to watch. It didn't take long before all eight fledged, all flying handily."

(See Donna's photograph, Plate 10.)

Fledging

Unless you are fortunate to actually see the fledglings leaving the nest box, you will have to depend on your records and observations from a distance to determine whether the nestlings have fledged. Parent bluebirds should be going to the box with food approximately every five minutes. If you have watched the box for some time without observing activity, place a small twig, leaf, even some spider webs across the hole , finish checking the rest of your trail, and return once more. If there is still no activity at the box, the light obstruction remains, and your notes tell you the young may have fledged, it's time to peek.

An empty nest will be flattened, with perhaps a remaining fecal sac or two. The exact date of fledging may be followed by a question mark in your records, but if nothing else remains in the nest, you will have to assume that those nestlings you last saw at age twelve or thirteen days have all fledged successfully.

The young exit one at a time. They can fly 100 feet or more to a perch, or may land on the ground and be ushered to cover by the parents, who will continue feeding them (sometimes only the male if the female is busy re-nesting) for several days. It will take at least a week or ten days for the young to learn the technique of capturing their own prey; a month to six weeks before they are independent.

Two days old

Dick Peterson

Four days old

Dick Peterson

PLATE *13*

Eight day old nestling

Mountain bluebird nestlings - NW Minnesota

PLATE 14

Ten day old eastern bluebird

Sixteen day
old eastern
bluebird

PLATE *15*

Jeff Stave

Twenty-three day old hand-raised eastern bluebirds

Speckled
like
robins

Dick Peterson

PLATE *16*

Male western bluebird removing fecal sack

Male eastern bluebird removes fecal sack

PLATE 17

Mountain bluebird ready to fledge from natural cavity

Mryna Pearman

Donna Hagerman

Four-five-week-olds from first brood visit box
of western parents and second brood of five

PLATE *18*

And they still have a lot to learn! Only about 50% of fledged bluebirds survive through migration to return as one-year -olds.

Once fledging is over, check the empty nest for parasites and also for clues as to what the young were being fed. Remove it some distance away so the smell won't attract predators, and lightly brush out the box. Do this immediately after each brood has fledged. Spraying an antiseptic into an empty box may make the monitor feel better, but there is little call for that, unless there is suspicion that blowfly eggs remain in the box.

Sometimes a new nest may already be started over the old one. In this case wait until egg laying has commenced and then remove the old nest and any old material or parasites from underneath the new nest. Leave enough nesting material to retain a padded cup, but second and third nests need not be deep.

Professor Wayne Davis of Kentucky has suggested that returning bluebirds preferentially select an old box that has not had the nesting material removed, when given a choice between that and an empty box. Attempts to duplicate those findings elsewhere have not substantiated this.

Avoidance or selection of the box is more likely due to earlier success in the box, rather than the fact the old nest is still there. Gowaty & Plissner found there was no significant effect in a study of 24 nests, half of which had not been cleaned out from a previous nesting. There were 24 nesting attempts in cleaned boxes, 26 in not-cleaned boxes. Equal numbers of both males and females returned to breed in cleaned and not-cleaned boxes the next breeding season....There was no significant effect of cleaning or not cleaning nest boxes on the chance of nestaing attempts or the numbers of nestlings fledged from nest boxes." (Gowaty & Plissner, 1997)

Monitors of the Hubert Prescott Trails near Portland Oregon found that when western bluebirds built over old nests, the additional nesting material brought the top of the nest too close to

101

the entrance hole, resulting in easy predation by jays, starlings and small raptors.(PWBRP Newsletter, Nov. '98)

Depending on the severity of winter conditions, blowflies may overwinter in old nests left in nestboxes. In cold climates they do not. The parasitic wasp of the blowfly is even more winter-hardy, which may seem to be a positive point for retaining the nest in the box if there have been blowfly problems. At this time, we still believe old nest removal is a good idea, both between nestings and between seasons. If you have had blowfly problems in the second nest, and believe a parasitic wasp may be present (see Chapter 6 - Problems), then either put the old nest in a wooded area where the wasp may winter over while the blowfly does not, or place the old nests in a tub or barrel, covered with a 1/8" mesh screen and place in a protected area such as a garage. Any over-wintering wasps will be able to escape to be of help next season.

House sparrows, tree swallows and violet-green swallows may be more likely to usurp a box with an bluebird nest than one without. One of the advantages of pairing boxes is that, when a bluebird tries to defend its box, swallows are more willing to settle for an the adjacent empty box.

Record Keeping

The importance of keeping records cannot be stressed too strongly. The manner in which the records are kept is up to individual preference, depending on what the monitor likes to carry on the trail, the mode of transportation, the number of nest boxes monitored, and, no less, the monitor's recall ability. Some middle-aged bluebirders, including this writer, will suddenly re-call a friend from third grade, but are lucky if we can remember what we left the room for! We must record details at each nest box along our trail at least weekly.

If we have seventy-five boxes scattered over three different trails, we must know the day when the box should be observed and not opened. We must know when the nestlings should have fledged. We must know if there really were five eggs when last checked, because now there are only three. We must know when to expect the eggs will hatch. Most important, we must know where there are other boxes with eggs or nestlings of similar ages so that if need be, we can foster out still-fertile eggs or orphaned nestlings. In addition, we may be able to help another bluebirder who needs that information.

In essence, we need to know exact dates, contents, and condition of each nestbox on the trail at all times. A small spiral notebook, with each page representing a nest box, may be tucked into a pocket. Some monitors prefer a clipboard with nest box numbers and location on one axis of a graph and dates on the other axis. Others may jot down abbreviated coded field notes and return home to enter all the information on a computer. Whatever the preferred method, information from the previous visit should be on hand each time the trail is checked.

Methods of identifying boxes vary. Numbers written directly on the wood with waterproof marking pen is sufficient if renewed periodically. Some bluebirders used stamped number dyes, others a woodburning tool. Metal numbers for wooden screens and storm windows may still be available in old-fashioned hardware stores. Even fancier, a metal stamping tool with dyes can be purchased

If nestboxes are paired, numbering them A and B when reporting nesting success may clarify records when they are compared to trails where nestboxes are spread far apart. Obviously the monitor with paired nestboxes can expect to fill only half the total nestboxes with bluebirds.

If you belong to a state, provincial or the national bluebird organization (NABS), sending your detail yearly reports, what you have observed and ideas that have helped you, will benefit all bluebirders. An annual directory of bluebirders, such as the one used by the Bluebird Recovery Program will also provide contacts for help when emergencies arise.

Maintenance

If you have front-drop or side-opening nestboxes and your area harbors house sparrows, field mice, or squirrels, you may prefer to leave the boxes open during the winter. If mice have been able to climb into your boxes, not only will they leave smelly excrement, but they may return after being thrown out in the spring and actually chew the young nestlings.

Otherwise, in late fall, you can close and adapt your nestboxes for overwintering beneficial songbirds - nuthatches, chickadees, titmice, downy woodpeckers, Carolina or Bewick's wrens, or even, if you are fortunate, bluebirds. Besides shutters, (described in Chapter 6 - Problems), the ventilation holes (and drainage holes) can be with fitted with wood plugs, duct tape, or flexible weather strip or other insulation to make them snug and inviting for roosting.

Whether the nest boxes are left closed or open over winter, they should be checked, cleaned if necessary, painted and repaired, and made ready for bluebird occupancy in early spring — from the first of March on, depending on latitude, altitude in the case of mountain bluebirds, and weather. Bluebirds seldom begin to nest immediately on arrival, but do inspect boxes long before they start seriously bringing in nesting material.

Late winter or very early spring is a good time to take note not only of boxes that need repair, roofs that need replacing, but also boxes that need to be moved around if that wasn't done in the fall.

Nestboxes erected in open public places or away from one's home can be vandalized. Substituting a Phillips-head screw for the nail, which allows the box to be opened easily, will foil the simply curious. Small signs covered with plastic can be stapled to the box as well, warning that tampering with the nestbox is a federal offense. The Bluebird Recovery Program of Minnesota has plastic signs like this for use (only in Minnesota). These offer a $100 reward for arrest *and conviction* of anyone tampering with the nestboxes, and a telephone number to report violations.

$100   REWARD

Bluebird nestboxes and contents are protected by State and Federal laws. If you have information lead- to the arrest and conviction of any- one vandalizing bluebird nestboxes and contents, call the Minnesota Department of Natural Resources and/or the U.S. Fish and Wildlife Service law enforcement agencies at 1-800-652-9093. The reward will be paid by the Minnesota Bluebird Recovery Program.

A Final Caution for the Monitor

While most bluebirders have seen their share of bothersome deerflies, blackflies, and ticks, the tiny deer tick, also called bear tick or rabbit tick (*Ixodes dammini*), may carry the spirochete bacteria *Borrelia burgdorferi* which causes Lyme disease. Origi- nally discovered in Connecticut, it is a serious threat all across the northern part of the continent to the northwest coast. The first symptoms —fever, headache, abdominal and joint pain, and a stiff neck may be mistaken for flu or arthritis. Circles of red rash may appear anywhere on the body three to thirty-two days after the bite, but one-third of those who contract Lyme disease do not develop the rash. Symptoms may disappear and recur intermittently for several months. Very serious arthritis, meningitis, neurologic problems, and cardiac problems may develop later.

Early treatment of Lyme disease is important because antibiotics such as tetracycline, penicillin, and erythromycin can cure the disease or lessen the symptoms if detected early. Two quick and accurate blood tests have recently been developed, one in New England and the other in Minnesota by 3M. The latter is called the *Fastlyme Test*. Domestic animals and dogs can also get Lyme disease and develop similar symptoms. (The vaccine for dogs was available long before a human vaccine.) Just recently, migrating birds, especially ground foraging ones , were found to carry the tick, originally though to infect only small wild rodents (such as deer mice) and white-tailed deer (*Odocoileus virginianus*).

The FDA has just (December 21, 1998) approved a Lyme vaccine, called Lymerix®. It is taken in three doses, the first two a month apart and the third one year later. It is expensive, but HMOs may cover it. However, (1) it is not 100% effective, (2) is not approved for children under 15, (3) does not work well for those over 70, (4) annual booster shots should be used, (5) there are some health conditions that make it advisable not to have the vaccine, (6) it does not protect against another potentially deadly tick-borne disease, human ganulocytic erlichiosis (HGE).

The best advice for those who could be exposed is PREVENTION. In any tick area, it's best to wear light-colored clothes, long pants tucked into socks, and shirts tucked into belts. Check every part of your body very carefully several times after being in the area. If the tick is removed with 12-24 hours, the chance of infection if Minimal, because it takes that long to transmit the spirochete. Most important, if any of the aforementioned symptoms appear, with or without the characteristic rash, after a positive diagnosis one can get successful treatment with antibiotics.

A repellent for clothing, called Permanone®, is very effective in both repelling and killing ticks. Its active ingredient is 0.5% permethrin. It is intended to be sprayed on clothing, not on skin. *Permikill®* for dogs is the companion product to *Permanone*. Other sprays containing pyrethrin have more recently become available.

Nymph
Most cases of Lyme disease are caused by the nymph, which looks like a freckle or speck of dirt. The nymph feeds from May through August.

Adult male and female
The larger adult ticks feed in late fall and early spring, but are easier to see and remove. After feeding on deer, the female lays her eggs.

Deer tick enlarged

Engorged tick
This is the size of a fully engorged adult female deer tick.

Wood ticks (also called dog ticks) are larger than deer ticks, have white markings on their back, and do not transmit Lyme disease.

There are at least two other possible hazards to bluebirders monitoring their boxes…:

Hanta virus has moved from being a remote possibility in the southwest to a real threat to people in many parts of the country who may inadvertently inhale the dust from mice nests and feces. It doesn't mean every mouse nest you remove will be infected, but precautions should definitely be taken before removing mouse nests: do not breathe in the dust, don't handle the nest with your bare hands. While Lysol® will not kill the virus, a 50/50 mixture of Lysol® and water can be used to spray down the mouse nest before you remove it, and once again inside the empty nestbox. Hanta virus is no joke. It can be fatal, and as yet there is no vaccine and no immediate positive medical procedure that will stop the virus before it stops you!

Obviously bluebirders are no more at risk of contracting the aforementioned diseases than anyone else who frequents the same areas, but a little planning, prevention and understanding will help make monitoring a safe as well as happy experience.

Finding Banded Birds

A more cheerful topic is the excitement of finding banded cavity nesters, "returns". Licensed banders capture and band birds by using mist nets, or box or ground traps. Monitors who wish to momentarily trap adult bluebirds in the box should wait until the parents are feeding young, a time when abandonment is least likely. Occasionally it is possible to gently lift an incubating female off eggs and read her band, but this should be done with great caution and only when you have determined by previous visits that she will not be unduly disturbed. Nestlings are best banded between 10 and 13 days of age, when their legs have less "baby fat", the legs are closer to their adult size, and sexes can be differentiated.

Band numbers should be sent to the National Biological Service, Bird Banding Laboratory, 12100 Beech Forest Road, Laurel, Maryland 20708-4037, or the numbers can be e-mailed to the lab: bbl@nbs.gov. You can go to their web site: http://www.pwrc.nbs.gov/bbl/800.htm or call toll free 1-800-327-2263. (*Note - e-mail and web sites change. Check the above references for current accuracy.*)

You need to report current condition of bird (live, dead, sick), when and where you obtained it. Include latitude and longitude if you can. Licensed banders will have sent all records to the lab, and they in turn will tell you when and where and at what age the bird was banded.

Knowing that one of your birds made it through the winter and is successfully nesting again or elsewhere is almost as thrilling as that first bluebird nest in your box!

Notes

Chapter 6

Competition and Usurpation

Other birds and small mammals find that bluebird nest boxes make good homes, too. Some may simply use an empty box; others take over or usurp the box for their own use, even though it may contain a bluebird (or other avian) nest, eggs, or young. More serious are the ones which not only usurp a box, but having claimed one, will destroy the contents of all other bluebird nestboxes not only in their own territory but even beyond—the avian competitor -predator.

To top these off, there are the pure predators — avian, reptilian, and mammalian—hungry for food, not housing. A list of these, starting at the bottom of the danger scale and ending with the worst, might scare off a beginning bluebirder. Luckily, each individual bluebird trail will probably have only one or two problems. All can be dealt with in some way or at least kept to a minimum, even though it may take several years of experimenting. This is another example of why exchanging ideas with other bluebirders can save a lot of time and frustration.

Mice, Chipmunks, Squirrels

Over the winter and into spring, white-footed mice (*Peromyscus spp.*), field mice (*Microtus spp.*), deer mice (*Peromyscus maniculatus*), chipmunks (*Tamias spp.*), red squirrels (*Tamiasciurus hudsonicus*) and flying squirrels (*Glaucomys volans*) may move in. The larger gray squirrels (*Sciurus carolinensis*) and fox squirrels (*Sciurus niger*), more likely urban dwellers, may find or chew a hole larger than the recommended 1½" or 1⁹/₁₆" round or 1³/₈" x 2¹/₄" oval one. Putting tacks or applying a thin metal shield around the circumference of the hole will prevent chewing. (Be sure the sharp metal doesn't overlap the hole.)

The mouse nest will likely consist of shredded milkweed pods, giving the appearance of cotton, with seeds and seedheads. Throwing everything out — mice and nest — and leaving the box open usually solves the problem. Be careful - that could cause problems for you (see end of *Chapter* 5 - Monitoring). But sometimes mice return as predators, eating eggs or chewing and killing nestlings. Climb-proofing the posts will stop them.

Squirrels and chipmunks usually fill the box with chewed bark and leaves. Once disturbed, they will move their young elsewhere. Moving the nest boxes away from trees and underbrush and climb-proofing the posts will stop their returning to gnaw on nestlings. Squirrels and chipmunks have killed nestlings and adult bluebirds in nest boxes and incorporated the carcasses into their nesting material.

Wrens

With the exception of the common house wren, most species in the same family (*Troglodytidae*) have rarely caused problems in bluebird nestboxes. The Bewick's wren is normally found in the west and southwest. It does not often use a nestbox. Dick Purvis of Southern California has had one Bewick's wren nest in his bluebird boxes in each of the last five years (to 1999). It may use some sticks, but also may have leaves, cotton, wool, pieces of snakeskin The cup may be lined with feathers or hair. They seem to be particular fond of nesting near water in the roots of trees and other low crevices and crannies. Dick Purvis's is the only report we know of that attributes to Bewick's wren the house-wren type of destruction of other species' nests in its territory. (Purvis, 1999) Bewick wren populations have deceased where house wrens have moved in. Neither Bewick's nor Carolina wren migrates seasonally like the house wren.

The Carolina wren, commonly known in the east and southeast, has been expanding its range northward. It falls back in harsh winters. In some of its new northern habitats, it has found well-maintained suet feeders and even black oil sunflower seeds a reliable winter sustenance. It is similar in appearance to the Bewick's, with a white eyeline, but has buff-color underneath where the Bewick's is white. It has nested in bluebird nestboxes of Darlene Sillick, Columbus, Ohio, (1999) In thick underbrush near moist areas, it sings an amazingly strong sweet three-note song. It nests twice a season. The nest will be of grass, weed stalks, inner bark, leaves, mosses, rootlets, and feathers, and sometimes pieces of snakeskin.

The house wren, covering the entire continent, is a different story. As early at the 1920s ornithologists warned about the profusion of nest boxes which people were putting around their homes and gardens to attract the beneficial insect-eating house wren (*Troglodtyes aedon*) which sang so beautifully. After encouraging their reproduction for 70 years, we now have the backlash of those efforts in the destruction and interference they may cause as they extend their territories into those of other

Because house wrens normally arrive later in the season, troubles starts near the second nesting of the bluebirds, but wrens may nest several times a season, The male wren will put small sticks in every box within his territory regardless of whether they are already occupied. He will defend the boxes until his mate makes her choice. In contrast to other bird species, the male wren will protect his territory (1/2 to 3/4 acre) against all other species rather than just another male wren.

In so doing he may clean out nests, eggs, and even young of all birds within his territory. The female will carry grass and feathers to make the cup on top of the one box of sticks she chooses. The small soft cup, high in the back, seemingly inaccessible, contains six small, pink, speckled eggs. Unfortunately,the female may also become predacious. These small birds not only may pierce bluebird eggs, leaving tiny holes, but can carry out whole eggs and young nestlings over a number of days. Even young unmated male wrens act similarly to the adult mated male, piling sticks into cavities and destroying other nests and contents. Kendeigh (1941) noted that the destruction may even involve the death of an adult bird.

Some years ago Dick Tuttle reported just 8% of bluebird nests had wren destruction in Ohio. When Linda Brown studied three years of recent Nebraska trail reports, she found the presence of wrens in 62% of the bluebird reports (1997-98). Of the 331 bluebird reports in Minnesota in 1997, 40% had wren problems. That percentage went down slightly in Minnesota in 1998 as monitors moved their boxes further and further into open areas.

Since wrens are protected birds, neither the soft cup nest on top of the sticks, the eggs, nestlings nor adults can not be harmed. It is legal, however, to remove the dummy sticks which the male wren puts in all the other boxes box before the female makes her choice and starts her nest.

The best solution so far has been to move bluebird nest boxes *at least* 200 feet from cover—dense brush, trees, or vines. Do not put up wren boxes along borders of trees and shrubs in hopes this will lure wrens away from bluebird boxes. It just add to the wren population and assures that more wrens will return again the next year. House wrens do not need artificial nestboxes — after years of being so supplied, they are surviving well— too well— already.

Contrary to popular commercially available wren house design, wrens really seem to prefer the larger bluebird entrance hole, though it may make them more susceptible to predation.

Wooden and wire wren guards of various designs have been tried. Unfortunately, boxes so equipped will be less attractive to bluebirds, so the monitor must be vigilant to attach the guards after the bluebird eggs have been laid. Bob Orthwein of Ohio has had success in attaching a wood block which extends from the edge of the overhanging nestbox roof to just past the bottom of the entrance hole. This has worked with chickadee eggs and in one instance he was able to protect bluebird eggs in this manner . Both the chickadee female and the bluebird female returned to incubate their eggs and successfully fledge their broods.

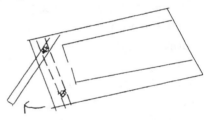

top view of Peterson box;; guard swings out after removing one of the two screws, so box front can be opened for checking.

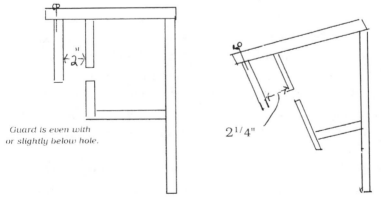

Guard is even with or slightly below hole.

$2^{1/4}$"

Orthwein -   Wren Guard

115

Chickadees

The Black-capped chickadee (*Parus atricapillus*), and the Carolina chickadee (*Parus carolinensis*) of the southeast, are beneficial birds, causing the bluebirds no harm, Both chickadee prefer boxes close to cover, even deep in the woods. Nesting sometimes twice a year, they will use a regular bluebird box placed at some distance from cover. The nest base is of fresh moss, over which a cup of soft fur is placed . The female pulls soft fur is over the small, white, red-spotted eggs when she leaves, even when her exit is hurried. Bluebird boxes are rarely available in the mountain chickadee's domain. The latter has a similar nest, with the fur being very soft — of mouse or squirrel.

The chestnut-backed chickadee is found only along the west coast of California, Oregon, Washington and Canada into Alaska. The Boreal chickadee only occasionally crosses south over the Canadian border.

Chickadees will also use nestboxes in winter for roosting. Plug all but the entrance hole, and tightly wedge several small sticks or dowels horizontally above the floor. They will also use roosting boxes.

Titmice

Titmice are in the same family as chickadees. The nest and eggs of a titmouse is very similar to the chickadee's, but the titmouse may also use strips of bark and leaves in the nest building and may actually cover the eggs with leaves rather than fur. The titmouse sometimes includes bits of snakeskin or cellophane. The four to eight white eggs are speckled in various degrees with reddish brown color.

Titmice do not migrate seasonally. The tufted titmouse (*Parus bicolor*) is native to the southeast, but also appears in southwest Wisconsin, northeast and southern Iowa, and southeast Minne-

Lois Nissen

The precocious child

John Thompson

The orphan named Mabel

PLATE *19*

Black-capped
chickadee
nestlings

Dick Peterson

Dick Peterson

Black-capped chickadee eggs

PLATE *20*

Tree
Swallow

Dick Peterson

Tree swallow nest and eggs

Dick Peterson

PLATE *21*

Egg comparisons; three starling, one robin, three bluebird, two bluebird, two house sparrow.

Bluebirds at mealworm feeder.

PLATE 22

sota. Its range is gradually extended northward, The oak titmouse *(Parus inornatus)*, also called plain titmouse, is fairly well restricted to oak woodlands in California and to a few pockets in the southwest states. Non-migratory, it may be an early user of bleubird nestboxes, and even squeeze into wren boxes. The female is usually reluctant to leave her chickadee-like nest with its white eggs during monitoring.

House Finches

The house finch male, or linnet *(Carpodacus mexicanus)*, is similar in appearance to a purple finch, though a little more slender and his red color appears to be red-orange. A western bird, illegally released in New York in 1940, it has spread astonishingly rapidly across the United States. It is reported to be the only bird which has met itself going both directions: the eastern advance of house finches met the western population at the Missouri River! First reported in Minnesota in 1876 as an accidental, it was not noted again until 1980, and now is in all 87 counties of Minnesota. They are remarkable adaptable everywhere. At this point (1999) the house finch does not appear to be a serious threat in displacing bluebirds, and in fact many reports suggest that house sparrows have declined where house finches have moved in. A recent contagious eye disease of house finches has spread from the eastern U.S. and has impacted populations of birds there.

The nest is usually on tree branches, on ledges, or in old oriole nests, but the finch has also used bluebird boxes, a transparent window seed feeder, hanging planters and even old Christmas wreaths.

The female builds the nest alone, of grass, debris, and slender dry stems, often with leaves attached. The four to five eggs are bluish white or creamy, or bluish-green with or without fine purple streaks. The nest with young is greatly soiled. They raise two or more broods.

Eurasian Tree Sparrows

Few bluebirders will ever see a Eurasian tree sparrow (*Passer montanus*), but Trish Quintenz has had them nesting in her Menard County, Illinois nestboxes. First introduced in St. Louis, Missouri in 1870, they are still restricted to those two states , save for a small group of them which are thought to be have nested in grain barges going up the Mississippi from St. Louis, going ashore near Burlington, Iowa (*Mn. Birding*, Jan-Feb. '96). They are members of the same weaverbird family as house sparrows and at first glance have a similar appearance, the male having a black throat patch but there is also a black eye patch above a whitecheek patch patch .

Woodpeckers

Occasionally woodpeckers (genus *Picidae*) and yellow-shafted flickers (*Colaptes auratus*) enlarge an entrance hole if the box is placed high, in or at the edge of woods; but only the small downy woodpecker will regularly use the box for nesting or for roosting in winter.

Nuthatches

Attracted to surroundings similar to those preferred by chickadees, the white-breasted nuthatch (*Sitta carolinensis*) makes its nest of small pieces of bark lined with grass, feathers, or animal hair. Vern Johnson (1998) observed a nuthatch taking fur from (regurgitated) owl pellets and burying it deep into the nest. The five to six eggs are white, speckled with red and brown. Laurance Sawyer (1988) observed chunks of mud brought to the nest box roof by nuthatches, broken into small pieces, and carried into the nestlings, though no evidence of mud remained after fledging. Male nuthatches also may smear dirt below the entrance hole both inside and outside of the box, and sometimes pitch is smeared below the hole. Perhaps this is a climbing predator deterrent? (Nuthatches enter the hole from above.)

The red-breasted nuthatch (*Sitta canadensis*), migratory across the continent, in contrast to the white-breasted nuthatch, usually excavates its own hole; the white-breasted rarely does. Both will use nest boxes in partly open wooded areas. The brown-headed nuthatch of the extreme southeastern U.S. also may use a nestbox. Its counterpart, the pygmy nuthatch of far western high altitudes has not been reported in an artificial cavity.

Nuthatches rarely compete with bluebirds because they prefer being in or close to wooded areas.

Prothonotary Warblers

The only cavity nester of the warblers, the prothonotary (*Protonotaria citrea*), has a range listed as the eastern half of the U.S., but has been seen variously across the country. Dr. Walter Breckenridge had one nesting in a Peterson box north of Minneapolis along the Mississippi River. (Unfortunately it was displaced by a squirrel.) It has also been seen at Point Reyes, on the California coast above San Francisco. Though it is listed as a critically-endangered species in Canada, it has nested in the wooded swamps along the north shore of Lake Erie, where tree swallows and wrens and cowbirds compete for cavities. Don Willis set up wooden and 4" PVC nestboxes, all camouflaged, with $1^3/8$" entrance holes, near the Long Point Observatory in Eastern Ontario. The prothonotary warbler chose the PVC box and the male seemed to be attracted to areas where several nestboxes were grouped together. Of 35 known prothonotary nests in Canada in 1997, one-half were in artificial nestboxes.

These beautiful yellow-headed warblers' natural nest is in the wooded swampy areas. They used a bluebird box just one foot above the water when the nested 1/4-mile from Washington D.C, near the state line with Maryland (Zyla & Donovan, 1993). They are also found in the wooded, flooded areas of the Mississippi River near Winona, Minnesota. Cowbird parasitism is the major

119

threat in natural cavities, but artificial nestboxes and regular monitoring could cause a turnaround for these beautiful at-risk warblers (Wills, 1998).

Flycatchers

Great crested flycatchers (*Myiarchus crinitus*) are also beneficial birds pressured by lack of housing. They like to be close to wooded areas. Unable to enter a standard bluebird hole, they will use a box if the entrance hole has been enlarged by squirrels or woodpeckers. Their nest is made of coarse grass and leaves and almost always a piece of snakeskin or plastic appears in the nest or hanging nearby, or possibly in both places. Edwin Way Teale (1974) noticed they sometimes substituted strips of cellophane for snake skin. The three to four large cream-colored eggs are irregularly and heavily splotched with deep purple. Great crested flycatchers pose no threat to bluebirds. They seem to hold their own with house sparrows, but starlings trouble them. If you wish to attract crested flycatchers, use a 2" diameter hole or if there are starlings in the vicinity, a 1⁹⁄₁₆" hole.

The smaller ash-throated flycatcher (*Myiarchus cinerascens*) of the west and southwest may complete with bluebirds during the second nesting. They spend winters in Central America and migrate north a little later. They will use a 1½" or a 1⁹⁄₁₆" entrance hole. Hatch Graham has had them nesting 12 feet from another (paired) bluebird-occupied box, and there has been no trouble (Graham, 1998).

Swallows

Though later in arriving, tree swallows (*Iridoprocne bicolor*) and violet-green swallows (*Tachycineta thalassina*) have in the past made more than one bluebirder across North America to give up hope of establishing a trail only for bluebirds. Sometimes their single nesting cycle will overlap with the first and second of the bluebird and, if there are enough boxes, all is well. They are not really competitors for food, because they are aerial feeders. They may even help keep house sparrows out of the area. But eventually, some year, the cycles will coincide and they will compete for and usurp bluebird boxes. They may build over a bluebird nest containing eggs and they have been known to puncture eggs and throw them out (Boone, 1980).

The tree swallow nest may initially look like the bluebird's, but of slightly coarser grass and weeds, and containing feathers, preferably white feathers which they continue to add during the nestling period. Their six oval, dull, pure-white eggs are slightly smaller than bluebirds eggs. Pairing of boxes usually solves the problem unless the population pressure has become so strong that they colonize like martins. If the bluebird trail is just getting started, and especially if it is near water, pair two boxes ten to twenty-five feet apart, with at least 300 feet to the next pair.

Berner (1998) concluded that the pairing as described works, but both species will benefit if the paired boxes are placed at longer intervals i.e. 300 feet. Boone found that tree swallows will rarely nest together as close as three feet, but prefer at least eight to ten-foot distances even when pressured. Dick Tuttle has many of his 100 nestboxes in central Ohio paired. There eastern bluebirds and tree swallows nest peaceably within 20-30 feet of each other. Tuttle also found that tree swallows defended the bluebird box as well as its own from house wrens and house sparrows. Carol and Dave Fiedler (1998) have banded, in the past 30 years, 10,000 tree swallows in mid-central Minnesota. A male tree swallow having two females in two separate boxes is rare there. The Fiedlers have observed it about once every seven years. Carol says, " Nature has provided for both birds [tree swallows and bluebirds] to survive [on our bluebird trails.]"

Because they depend mostly on flying insects, cold rainy spells are harder on tree swallows than on bluebirds. By 1992 tree swallow populations has dropped to a 10-year low. Like some other birds, they tend to have population cycles, of perhaps 10 years duration.

Tree swallows are sometimes mistaken for purple martins (Progne subis). Both male and female tree swallow are white underneath, with backs of iridescent greenish-blue. Martins are larger, the male all bluish-black ("purple"), the female dusky underneath. There has not been a confirmed martin nesting in a bluebird box, though the reverse is true—bluebirds have occupied martin houses.

Like tree swallows, violet-green swallows (*Tachycineta thalassina*) of the far west, from the Rockies to the west coast and into Alaska, have an almost iridescent back, wings and tail. They are distinquished from tree swallows by their white rump.

One of the added bonuses in the joy of bluebirding is the fun of throwing feathers up into the area near nesting swallows, and waching them dive and catch the feathers in mid-air. They have even been coaxed to retrieve them from outstretched fingers. Swallows will continue to add feathers during the nestling stage.

In areas where both tree swallows and violet-green swallows may compete for bluebird nestboxes, triple boxing can help. The late Earl Gillis of Oregon found this worked well, especially if he placed some of the bluebird boxes on large trees with overhead branches. This gave the bluebirds an advantage in defending their boxes against the more aerial acrobatic swallows. Both species of swallows have been known to assist in the feeding of eastern and western bluebird nestlings.

Note: All the above birds are native to North America, beneficial, and federally protected. It is illegal to destroy them, their nests, or their eggs.

Starlings

Starlings (*Sturnus vulgaris*), introduced on the east coast in the 1880's, have become very serious competitors and predators of bluebirds and other native birds using natural tree cavities. The average-sized adult starling cannot completely enter a 1 $1/2$" or a 1$9/$16" round hole (Zeleny, 1969). In the northern part of the continent starlings would not normally choose to nest in a small Peterson box with a 1$3/8$ x 2$1/4$" oval hole or a Gilbertson PVC box with even smaller interior dimensions, but they can squeeze through or may partially enter and kill or carry out nestlings. Keith Kridler of Texas has found Peterson fronts on deeper boxes are attractive to southern starling. Starlings in the south are more slim than northern starlings, as is true of other animals (Zeleny, 1987). They can enter a slot-front box if the hole is 1$1/2$ x 5 inches . (McComb et al.,1987).

Their grass nest is similar to a bluebird's, but of coarser materials, and the eggs are a similar shape and blue color, though larger. Starlings are not protected. They are partially responsible for the bluebirds' decline, driving them from tree cavities. Shooting is certainly permissible. Trapping in the nest box is similar to that for house sparrows. Communal birds, they usually stay in family groups, especially in winter, and winter is a good time to attract them to suet-baited ground traps.

House Sparrow

There is one other competitor and usurper which is an even more deadly predator —the worst avian enemy of bluebirds, which many bluebirders would firmly state is the worst of all predators. The house sparrow, formerly known as the English sparrow (*Passer domesticus*), is a deadly predator. His predatory behavior is dicussed in Chapter 7. Confirmation of its nest in the bluebird box it has usurped gives warning that predation of young bluebirds may be imminent.

The experiments of Wayne Davis (1998) indicate that house sparrows are especially attracted to round entrance hole with a predator guard. The research of others has not confirmed a definite design to be more enticing. Undoubtedly the predator guard provided the perch the house sparrow does like. Dean Sheldon of Ohio has found sparrows are attracted to a box that has some grass already sticking out the entrance hole, a factor Dean uses in luring them for the trapping. The first clue to sparrow trouble is often the sight of wisps of grass actually sticking out the nest box entrance or vent holes or from cracks in the box. The loose nest inside is composed of rough grasses, weeds, hair, feathers, and often pieces of junk—plastic, cigarette butts, and so forth. The nest is domed over the entrance hole, but the five to seven eggs, white spotted with brown are visible. Sometimes the background color of the eggs appears faintly gray-green or bluish.

This alien bird is neither federally nor state protected, and must be severely dealt with on any bluebird trail. If you cannot manage to do so, you should not start a bluebird trail or even one or two nestboxes. You will be doing more harm than good for our native songbirds.

Some potential bluebird nestbox occupants

Nesting Activities		Bluebirds	Tree Swallows	House Wrens	House Sparrows
Dates:	Earliest arrival	So MN: 2-22, No MN: 3-6	So MN: 3-12, No MN: 3-22	So MN: 3-30, No MN: 3-30	Permanent resident
	Peak arrival	Mid March to mid April	Mid to late April	Early May	Permanent resident
	Breeding season†	Mid April to early May	Mid May	Early May to early June	Mid April to early May
	Peak departure	Late Sept to late Oct	August & September	Early September	Permanent resident
	Location of nest (in natural cavities)	Open country with scattered trees to wood borders, near mowed or sparsely covered ground.	Partly open country with old or dead trees, often near water	Open woodland & wood borders, shrubland, farmland, suburbs, up to 200' from cover	Hole or crevice anywhere, especially by buildings
	Male claims nest with	Grass (1-6 weeks before nest building)‡	Curved white feathers	Twigs with spider egg cases§	Grass or by sitting in hole§
Nest Building:	Materials	Dry grass & weed stems, pine needles (occasionally fine rootlets or twigs), lined with finer grass (occas. hair or feathers)	Dry grasses (occasionally straw, cattails or pine needles), lined with feathers (often white)	Twigs with spider egg cases (occasionally stems, leaves, fibers), lined with fine grass, feathers, hair, bark strips	Long coarse grass stems with seed heads, weeds, feathers, trash
	Size & shape	Loosely built with 2-3" cup	Loosely woven with large shallow cup, feathers upright curving over eggs	Bulky base of twigs (nearly filling box) with small deep cup at top rear	Large untidy dome with side entrance to deep space with little or no bottom
	Days to build and builder	4-11 days usually, by F, -M (2-14 days possible) + possibly 1+ week before first egg laid	14-21 days usually, by F (7-30 days possible)	M: 8-10 days (base) + F: 4 days (lining) + possibly 2 days before 1st egg laid	1+ days, by M, -F
Eggs:	Color (size)	Blue to white, somewhat glossy (21x16mm)	White, slightly glossy to non-glossy (19x13mm)	Light pink to white with rust specks (16x12mm)	Off-white to bluish green w/ gray brown spots (23x16mm)
	Total number laid	4-6 eggs (3-7 possible)	5-6 eggs (4-8 possible)	5-8 eggs (to 12 possible)	4-6 eggs (3-8 possible)
	Incubation period	12-14 days (12-18 days possible)	14-15 days (13-16 days possible)	13 days (12-15 days possible)	12 days (10-14 possible)
	Hatch timing	Synchronous	Synchronous (or partially asynchronous)?	Synchronous	Synchronous
DO NOT DISTURB after: Nestlings could prematurely fledge.		12 days	15 days	9 days	Remove eggs before they hatch!!
Total Time in Nest:		17-18 days usually (15-20 is possible)	20-21 days usually (16-24 possible)	16-17 days usually (12-18 possible)	15-16 days usually (14-17 possible)
Number of Broods:		2 broods (sometimes 3)	1 brood (rarely 2)	1-2 broods (rarely 3)	2-3 broods (sometimes 4)

* Dates for southern Minnesota unless otherwise noted.
† When first egg is laid.
‡ Male claims several possible nest sites, but female makes the final selection.
§ Male or female may select site.
** M or F preceded by - indicates lesser involvement.

Chart by Rosanne Pankonin

Notes

Chapter 7

Predators and Problems

A list of every possible predator or problem on a bluebird trail would likely dissuade any would-be bluebirder. However, if you are willing to spend a little effort and perhaps a little expense to mount nestboxes safely, choose good boxes to put in a good location, and monitor regularly, you've got the best possible chance of having a successful, rewarding bluebird trail. It's an experience — a continual one — you'll never forget, never regret, and forever enjoy.

But you, and indeed we "old-timers," may get one or two of the unpleasant surprises described herein. The suggested solutions should help.

The House Sparrow (*Passer domesticus*)

Once you experience the carnage created by house sparrows, you know why all bluebirders must take the oath: "I will not, under any circumstances, allow house sparrows to nest in my boxes." Actually a European weaver finch rather than a New World sparrow, the house sparrow is probably the most frustrating predator to trap. The oft-repeated phrase, "Let Nature take its course," can be countered with the reminder that deliberate, repeated introduction of this bird into North America was not "Nature's way." It is possible that bluebirds could have survived, albeit in diminished numbers, the destruction of woodlands, the

127

removal of dead trees, and even man-made chemicals, were it not for that even earlier mistake of man.

Sadly, it is very difficult to convince people that those "cute little sparrows," cheerfully chirping all winter at the feeder and taking over untended martin houses, are anything but cute and cheerful—that they not only reduce the food available to beneficial song birds, they are vicious killers!

Few bluebirders have been able to prevent the competition and usurpation of nest boxes without also experienced the predation that is instinctive to house sparrows. Efforts to prevent them from using nest boxes range from lining the back of the box with foil, to lowering the box dangerously close to the ground (in the mistaken belief that they won't use a low box), to adding a stake with colored streamers , to attaching mylar strips or wire or cords closely spaced around the front of the box. Constantly removing the nest and eggs of this unprotected species can backfire. The sparrows may retaliate!

Only in an area new to house sparrow encroachment will these efforts be sufficient. More often they work the first year or two, only to suddenly turn to tragedy. The bluebird nest with healthy plump nestlings just getting their colorful pinfeathers is found on the next check to contain horrid, smelly, fly-ridden, bloody, mutilated corpses! Nothing is more heart-breaking on the bluebird trail. The sparrows thought to be getting along fine with the bluebirds have struck, seizing the opportunity when both parents were away foraging for food. Or a female bluebird which had been incubating five beautiful eggs or brooding newly hatched nestlings one day is found dead, hardly recognizable—eyes pecked out, head feathers gone, gashes in the skull—on top of five cold eggs or dead nestlings! The sparrows may already have built their own nest over the decaying body and the eggs or nestlings.

In order to deal successfully with the onslaught from the house sparrow, we need to know something of its natural history, its instincts, and its usual behavior.

Natural History. House sparrows were released at various places along the eastern seaboard between 1850 and 1870. Familiar to many of the new immigrants, who mistakenly thought that insects were the main diet of the birds and thus they would help eradicate crop pests, it took just twenty-five years to recognize house sparrows were much worse pests. By then it was too late: they quickly proliferated across the United States, following settlement and even getting ahead of it along the earliest railroad lines where boxcars spilled grain. They soon also became notorious for the destruction they cause among blossoms of various fruits (Teale 1978) and the spread of noxious weeds such as crabgrass.

They may well now be the most abundant wild bird species in North America (Beimborn, 1967), and the most successful wild bird in the world (Grussing, 1980). Eighty percent have at least two broods per season (Weaver, 1943) and in the more temperate areas will have three to five broods.

No true sparrow will attempt to use a bluebird box. (It's unfortunate that this bird, acutally the weaver finch, as mentioned carries the name of sparrow.) There should be no mistake in identifying the male. Although there is more individual variation in the male plumage than in most other wild bird species, his distinguishing features are: about 5¼ " long, a black bib and eyeline, white cheeks and white unstreaked underparts, chestnut-colored back, wings, and tail. There is some barring on the back and wings and faint white wing bars. The female is more likely to be confused with other female sparrows. She has an unstreaked dingy breast, bold, buffy eye line, and lightly-streaked back.

In his Master's thesis, Don Beimborn (1967) provides some very interesting clues to house sparrow behavior. They are not seasonally migratory birds, but generally spread out as a flock to areas not more distant than 1½ to 2 miles. Truly the farmer's enemy, they may go up to three miles to feed in ripening grain fields. "Perhaps the English sparrow is unique in that its mobility away from a roosting-feeding area is limited" (Beimborn). A territory occupied by a flock may encompass several sets of farm buildings. A bond seems to exist between individuals in a typical flock of from fifteen to a hundred birds, yet when stressed or trapped will kill their own kind..

As Beimborn points out, house sparrows in rural areas are attracted to livestock feed and droppings, especially near cattle feed lots. They depend on buildings and structures for roosting, nest sites, and cover. It's not surprising that, in establishing bluebird trails, especially those within one to three miles of farms, we are in effect enticing house sparrows. We are providing them with two of their three necessities (roosting cover and nest sites). In addition, they compete with bluebirds in foraging for soft insects for their nestlings.

While the territory occupied by a flock of house sparrows may cover several sets of farm buildings, and there is movement between nearby farms, the individual male's territory is limited to a small area around the nest. He may place debris in as many as five boxes, and may even carry two of the nests to completion. But the important thing to remember when trying to trap and eliminate house sparrows from the bluebird trail is that the bond between the male and the nest box he has finally chosen is stronger than the bond between the male and his mate. Having decided on his territory and a particular box, he remains attached to that box no matter what happens to the nest, eggs, or female. He quickly finds a replacement if his first mate disappears.

This bond between the male house sparrow and his nest box is amply described in Don Grussing's excellent small paperback book, *How to Control House Sparrows* (1980). Grussing points out that the attachment of the male house sparrow to his chosen site often begins before migrating birds arrive in the spring. This is another reason that sparrows are so hard to discourage. "You can kill (or trap) his mate, and" [in contrast to bluebird, chickadee, and tree swallow pairs, who move elsewhere once trouble has occurred] "the male sparrow will stay with the house he has selected. You can destroy his nest every day, and he will return often until the end of the breeding season, rebuilding the nest, 'chir-ruping' for a female all day long throughout the summer until finally his gonads have shrunk and he no longer remembers why he's singing." (Grussing). The female who loses her male will move on in search of another mate and nest site, but the lone male will stay and try (and usually succeed) in attracting another female to the site to which he is so attached.

Sparrow Traps. More than one bluebirder has come up with the idea of putting a mousetrap on top of a house sparrow nest in a bluebird box, after flattening the nest down so it doesn't interfere with the trapping mechanism. The standard mousetrap rarely actually catches the male or female, although it may scare the female away and the male enough to move over to another nest box where he will start again. Even if he does start over again elsewhere, he may "hold" the box from which he was frightened without ever re-entering it. This does not solve the problem.

Glue-type mouse traps are sometimes employed. If there were some way to be absolutely sure that the only bird which would be trapped and held in this inescapable glue, it might be recommended, The box must be watched constantly, without taking your eyes off it even for a moment. Other beneficial birds, even bluebirds, have entered a box containing a sparrow nest. If you are close enough to scare off that bird, the chances of a house sparrow not observing you and shying away, are slim. The bluebirder who has had to deal with a bluebird stuck into that trap will never do it again. And the bird will probably not survive after loosing so many feathers in the glue. It is not a humane way to dispose of any

131

creature, bird or mouse.

One easy, but not always successful, method of controlling the house sparrow population is to let them nest and then remove the house sparrow eggs every three to four days. If the nest is undisturbed, they may keep possession of the box and continue producing eggs, leaving other nestboxes alone. An alternative would be to addle (shake) the eggs, hoping the female continues incubation and not realize they won't hatch. It may work in a small area where sparrows are few.

Eradication is the only solution that really works! And constant eradication may be necessary over several years before all sparrow threats are taken care of. It is essential to trap and destroy the male house sparrow, even though it is far easier to catch the female. Catching the female is usually more easily done at dusk or at night when she is incubating eggs. The best time to catch the male is when the nest is being constructed, as it is the male who does most of the nest building.

Dick Peterson developed a substitute sparrow-trap front for the Peterson nest box some years ago, and in 1988 simplified it so that there are no visible trap wires visible outside that might "spook" the sparrow, making it so cautious that the bluebird trail monitor may give up waiting. The front be dropped down so the front-door-trap can be substituted. House sparrows are extremely wary: if the new door is different in color or stain, it is less likely to fool them. Joe Huber of Ohio, the late Vince Bauldry of Wisconsin, and others have developed similar, lighter traps that work from the inside of the regular front, a big advantage. (See Appendix.)

The Universal Sparrow Trap by Steve Gilbertson of Aitkin is simple, inexpensive and lightweight. It fits any wooden or PVC nestbox. It is constructed of a piece of steel measuring tape, a piece of oak trim, and some 12-gauge wire. (See diagram.)

House
wren
sticks

Steve Mortensen

After a house wren's visit

Dick Peterson

PLATE *23*

The blowfly (*Protocaliphora sialia*)

Blowfly lavae and pupae

PLATE 24

House wren - competitor and predator

Wren eggs and nest, above the sticks

PLATE *25*

Dick Peterson

House sparrow female and male

House
sparrow
eggs and
nest

Dick Peterson

PLATE 26

House sparrow's beak - a vicious tool

Dick Peterson

The house sparrow has been at work

Dick Peterson

PLATE 27

House sparrow
nest in
Peterson box

Dick Peterson

Starlings are
competitors
also

Dick Peterson

PLATE 28

One a day x 50 million U.S. cats =
4.4 million songbirds <u>per day</u>!

Paper wasp nest

PLATE 29

After the alfalfa was sprayed. (Mountain bluebird)

Dick Peterson

Jack Finch

A problem - especially in the south

PLATE 30

Noel
guard
with
adapter

John Thompson

Dick Peterson

That ol' frustrated feeling

PLATE *31*

Double
protection

Jack Jensen

PVC pipe
climbing
guard

Richard Simonsen

PLATE *32*

The Universal Sparrow Trap

GILBERTSON UNIVERSAL SPARROW TRAP

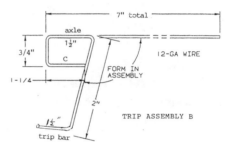

12-GA WIRE

FORM IN
ASSEMBLY

|←1-1/4→|

5/8

A

1"

HOOK MECHANISM A
for PVC boxes

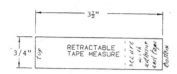

3½"

3/4" | RETRACTABLE
TAPE MEASURE

Tape measure piece extends
2&1/8" above top of oak
Secure with construction
adhesive & electrical tape.

Top of tape should
be wound with electri-
cal tape to soften
sharp edge.

7" total

axle

1½"

3/4"

C

FORM IN
ASSEMBLY

12-GA WIRE

1-1/4

2"

1¼"

trip bar

TRIP ASSEMBLY B

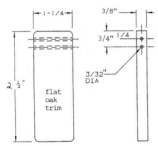

|←1-1/4→|

3/8"

3/4" | 1/4

3/32"
DIA

2½"

flat
oak
trim

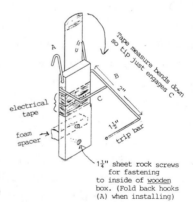

A

U

Tape measure bends
so tip just engages C

B

2"

1½"

trip bar

electrical
tape

foam
spacer

Side view of oak trim
Drill two 3/32" holes
through to other edge
for hook axle and axle
bar of trip assembly.

1¼" sheet rock screws
for fastening
to inside of wooden
box. (Fold back hooks
(A) when installing)

133

The traps are set as the monitor walks the bluebird trail, and are checked before leaving the area. When the Universal trap is sprung, a bright orange circle drawn or pasted on the trap's door will indicate the blocked entrance hole. It will be visible from some distance.

If there is difficulty reaching into the trap to grab the sparrow, a large clear plastic bag put over the entire box prevents the sparrow from flying to freedom. A small can with both ends removed and one end covered by a small plastic bag or mesh secured by a rubber band, or a clear plastic bottle with the top cut off, may be held to the entrance hole as it is opened. A branch or long twig pushed through the ventilation hole may convince the sparrow he had better exit.

Never leave the sparrow trap unattended for more than a few hours —it may cause the death of any bird deprived of food and water.

Trapping of house sparrows should continue all year, not just on the bluebird trail. There are several ground traps and trap plans available which catch and hold many sparrows at once (see Appendix). It is much easier to catch house sparrows in winter in the north, where snow cover leads the sparrows to traps baited with white bread crumbs, cracked corn, or millet. Always leave one or two captives in the cage as decoys to attract more house sparrows into it.

If you are reluctant to promptly and humanely dispatch these vicious, unprotected birds, another bluebirder who has suffered their depredation is usually willing to do so. Alternatively, a nearby falconer or rehabilitation center for raptors may welcome live food.

Hawks

Are hawks a serious problem on the bluebird trail? A few bluebirders each year report repeated trouble with kestrels, also called sparrow hawks (*Falco sparverius*). Long-time bluebirder Bob Smith of Shakopee, Minnesota, has trouble every year, especially in the beginning of the nesting season. Others have reported kestrels nesting within visual range of bluebird boxes with no problems.

Literature on the subject, documenting studies, reflects a similar inconsistency. The answer is simply that kestrels can and sometimes will take adult bluebirds and fledglings (Havera, 1983). The difference between <u>can</u> and <u>will</u> depends on pressure and stress. With all predators, hunger is the strong dictator, and convenience a secondary factor. Bluebird nestlings up to nine days old are particularly susceptible to being snatched from the nest box as they will reach up to be fed when there is activity at the entrance hole, while older nestlings flatten down to avoid danger (Steffen, 1981).

Once kestrels find ready prey, they may become conditioned to bluebird fare. However, according to a USDA study of 5,185 hawk stomachs, insects make up 63.5% of a kestrel's diet, rats and mice 20.3%, frogs and snakes 7.5% and small birds 8.4%. The kestrel small-bird diet, it should be noted, also consists of a large number of house sparrows, and in fact, in a study done by James Bryan (1988), house sparrows were the best bait in luring kestrels to traps in order to color band them.

Next in line on a hawk-threat list is Cooper's hawk (*Accipiter cooperii*) and sharp-shinned hawk (*Accipiter striatus*). Small birds make up 55% of a Cooper's hawk diet (and 12% of those are house sparrows) and 96.4% of a sharp-shinned hawk's diet. Neither of these birds, nor the northern harrier (*Circus cyaneus*), formerly called marsh hawk, whose diet is 41% small birds, can pluck nestling bluebirds from a nest box. These three hawks have such a wide range of hunting grounds that predation around a single bluebird trail is not usually a continuous problem. The diet of the red-tailed hawk (*Buteo jamaicensis*) is roughly 9% small

What Hawks Eat

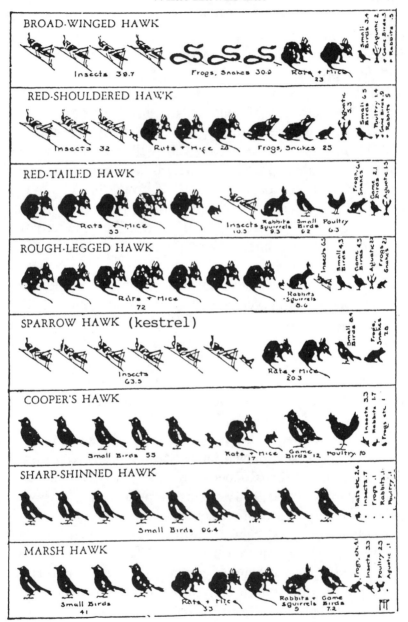

birds. The list could go on, but serious hawk predation is reported on only about one bluebird trail in twenty.

We need to reflect that some predation is part of Nature's scheme. And some of the predators are themselves rare and beautiful and necessary in the balance. This concept may be difficult to accept when it happens on <u>our</u> bluebird trail!

Other Avian Predators

The loggerhead shrike (*Lanius excubitor*) and occasionally the northern shrike (*Lanius ludovicianus*), both rare, will prey on small birds. House wrens, competitors and usurpers as well as predators, are described in the previous chapter. Later arrivals, they usually interfere more with a second bluebird nesting. They may throw out live nestlings over a number of days.

Tree swallows and violet-green swallows have rarely been incriminated as predators on young bluebird nestlings. More frequently they are merely competitors or usurpers. Birds of the jay family (*Cyanocitta*), and kestrels and starlings can intrude far enough into shallow bluebird boxes without exterior predator guards to pick out a nestling. Blue jays as well as common grackles (*Quiscalus quiscula*) will take advantage of any injured or partially helpless bird.

European starlings, like house sparrows unprotected by law, are most aggressive competitors. If the entrance hole is outsized, they will attack eggs, young and adult bluebirds. While house sparrows are the worst avian enemy of bluebirds in nest boxes, starlings are their worst avian enemies in natural cavities, and are in fact the main reason bluebirds have been driven from wooded areas. Very few natural cavities have entrances of such size that bluebirds can enter but starlings cannot. Like house sparrows, starlings are destroyers of fruit and other crops as well. A large wire and wood ground trap, with a larger slot than that for house sparrows, should be used if starlings are in the area.

Cowbirds, (*Molothrus ater*), which neither make their own nest nor raise their own young, will occasionally get into a bluebird box to deposit their eggs if the hole is large enough. They are much more likely to do so in a natural cavity or open nest of other birds.

Climbing Predators

Raccoons Raccoons (*Procyon lotor*), extremely intelligent mammals, frequently are predators of bluebird eggs, young birds, and even of the adult female on the nest. Raccoon predation can happen anytime, but is more likely to occur near
water, early in the spring, or in drought years, when their aquatic fare is lacking. Not only are they able to reach in through the entrance hole, they are strong and dexterous enough to pull out a loose screw or nail holding the box shut.

Hatch Graham, bluebirder, and breeder/trainer of search dog, deflates the theory that human scent leads the raccoon to a nestbox: *"Bunk! A raccoon is seeking birds to eat, and believe me, he can smell a bird in a box. He may well follow the trail we've walked because we've mashed down the grass. Most animals follow 'game' trails in their foraging. The bird's scent falls to the ground and 'pools' under and around the nestbox. High boxes are slightly more difficult for the scenting predator to pinpoint.*
"People have tried hanging mothballs and other items from nestboxes to confuse or mask the scent from a predator. A waste of time... Don't worry about leading a predator to the nestboxes. They can find them very well without help, thank you...." (Graham, 1997)

If one raid is successful, raccoons will continue investigating all boxes they come across in their territory, human scent or not.

Trapping and removing one raccoon only postpones the time when other raccoons move in to occupy the vacant territory.

Active nests and even entire nestboxes can be moved. The trail monitor must decide whether it is better to expose the female bluebird, eggs, or young to cat or raccoon predation in a badly-mounted nest box or to have both parents safe and possibly renesting somewhere else. Remember, bluebirds are less likely to abandon nestlings than eggs.

Six different exterior cat/coon guards were described in Chapter 4, most based on preventing the animal from putting its paw in, around, and down into the nest. Ideally, every nest box should be mounted so that it is impossible for climbing predators to get to the box in the first place. A predator-proof mounting is preferable to cat/coon guards on the nest box itself. Adult blue-birds, instinctively knowing they have to work harder, will choose a simple entrance hole over a longer one if they have that alternative (Bacon, 1989; Read, 1988). Unfortunately, climb-proof poles or pole-mounted guards may entail greater expense if the bluebird trail monitor has access only to new material.

Boxes should be at least five feet above ground. Ideal mounts include: smooth metal pipe, at least 1" in diameter, sprayed with a silicone spray like AmorAll® or completely enclosed by 2" square plastic or baked enamel downspout; and 1¹/2" PVC that has been rubbed with steel wool and coated with carnauba car wax. Two-inch square downspout will also cover T-post mounts. A 36" section of narrow PVC pipe mounted below the box over the post also stops many climbers.

Metal stovepipe, chimney flues, or short metal collars on wooden posts will not positively stop raccoons (or snakes or squirrels) from climbing, grasping, and encircling, although it may stop some cats. Raccoons have gone up heavily greased wooden posts. Long carpet-tack strips initially discourage raccoons but they have been known to return, evidently deciding sore paws were worth the dinner above. Commercial round wooden posts must be wrapped absolutely tightly with large sheets of overlapping tin, leaving no dents.

Cats (*Felis catus*) pose an equally serious threat to bluebirds. Whether a well-fed pet or a feral feline, cats are instinctive killers. In a study of seventy domestic cats in England, Churcher and Lawton (1987) found that over one-third of their prey were birds, and this represented twenty-two different species. The actual numbers were undoubtedly higher, as the count represented only those prey brought home and found by owners. Even on farms, only half of the prey was brought home.

Dr. Stanley Temple and John Coleman of the University of Wisconsin, Madison, projected figures from six farm cats to estimate 137 million songbirds killed annually by free-roaming cats in Wisconsin. The figures do not include city cats! Relate these Wisconsin figures to the estimate of *55 million* cats in the contiguous United States. Perhaps 10 per cent do not go outside; another 10 per cent may be too old or too slow; that still leaves *44 million*! If only one cat in ten of these kills a bird a day, the daily toll would be *4.4 million songbirds per day!*

Cat owners who cannot confine or leash their pets during the nesting season can trim the front claws to prevent cats from snaring young from the box or adults who are dive-bombing it. This does not prevent cats from climbing trees, nor catching birds on the ground. Itinerant cats should be disposed of. They can carry disease. Prevention of cat predation is the same as for raccoons — cat/coon guards or, preferably, climb-proof poles. Cats are good jumpers. They can jump as high as eight feet from a hard surface, less from sand or grass. (Bower, 1999). Unfortunately, house sparrows seem more adept than beneficial birds at avoiding becoming cat prey.

Others

Opossums (*Didelphis marsupialis*), weasels (*Mustela} spp*.), and skunks (*Spilogale putorius* and *Mephitis mephitis*) are occasional evening raiders of nest boxes also. They can be stopped from climbing by means similar to those for raccoons.

Mice (*Peromyscus spp.*) allowed to nest in boxes over the winter may return to eat eggs and young nestlings. The white footed mouse, or deer mice, are the species most likely to be found in nestboxes. They can be the carriers of Hanta virus. If possible, wet down their nest first, then use a plastic bag inverted over your hand to enfold the nest and remove it. Be careful to not inhale any dust from the nest. Lysol or clorox- diluted spray can be used to wet down the nest before removing it, but that does not kill the Hanta virus. Mice cannot climb smooth greased posts.

Attaching double-sided carpet tape or spreading grease or a product such as Tangle Foot® on the posts will leave clues to mammalian climbing predators (Davis, 1988). Mixing red cayenne pepper with grease before applying it to the poles may help the raccoons remember, for they will find themselves with hot tongues when cleaning themselves, but grease is not a long-lasting protection. Ropel® on posts may work, but also needs constant reapplication.

Snakes can climb smooth poles, even greased ones. Bull snakes, black snakes, and rat snakes take eggs and nestlings without leaving a clue as to what caused the disappearance. They prefer young, unfeathered nestlings and are more likely to be found in areas with mice and moles, or close to the edges of woods.

None of the snake repellents on the market now (1999) are effective. Usually they are a mixture of naphthalene (moth ball crystals) and sulfur. Recommended to repel several nuisance species from mice to skunks, they do not repel snakes. If snakes are the only predators in the area, flat metal squares of 24" hardware cloth under the box have proved effective for some (Cousineau and Morse, 1986). Wide circles of layers of garden netting has worked for others. A large inverted plastic bucket under the nest box will stop small snakes. (Be sure hole in the inverted bottom fits the pole fits tightly. The bucket is supported by brackets on the post.)

The device of Ron Kingston, of Charlottesville, Virginia, has worked successfully. (Kingston, 1991)

Stovepipe Predator Baffle

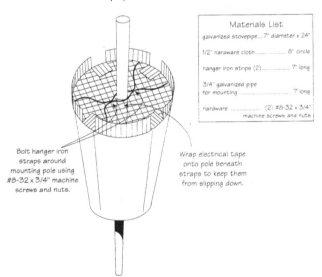

Materials List

galvanized stovepipe.... 7" diameter x 24"

1/2" haraware cloth............. 8" circle

hanger iron strips (2)................. 7" long

3/4" galvanized pipe
for mounting .... 7' long

hardware .... (2) #8-32 x 3/4"
machine screws and nuts

Bolt hanger iron straps around mounting pole using #8-32 x 3/4" machine screws and nuts.

Wrap electrical tape onto pole beneath straps to keep them from slipping down.

Using tinsnips, shape hardware cloth into a circle. Make a small cut in the center so it will slip over the mounting pole. Bend the edges of the hardware cloth down and slide it snugly into the stovepipe. Cut four tabs on the top end of the stovepipe. Bend them inward, over the hardware cloth.

Bolt the hanger iron straps together in the center, around the mounting pole. Bend the free ends outward to support the hardware cloth. A few wraps of electrical tape below the strap attachment will keep it from slipping down the pole. Slide the stovepipe assembly over the top of the mounting pole, resting it on the hanger straps. Attach the nest box onto the pole, with the bottom of the box about six inches above the top of the baffle. Smear bearing grease on the pole beneath the baffle to repel ants.

Plan design by Ron Kingston. Sialia 13(2): 56–57.

Parasites and Insects

The bluebird **blowfly** (called *Apaulina sialia* or *Protocaliphora sialia*) is the most serious parasite of bluebird nestlings, with the gnat or blackfly a close second. A Canadian Wildlife Study (1994) noted that blowflies were the most important nest loss factor; wrens were second and house sparrows the third most common cause of nest box failure. Usually neither the blowfly larvae sucking the blood nor the bite of the smaller flies actually causes death, but with large infestations the nestlings can be succumb to malnutrition or cold.

In June or July eggs are laid by the female blowfly in the nesting material and hatch into half-inch pale-grey larvae or maggots. These larvae attach to the nestlings to suck blood, especially at night, hiding in the nesting material during daylight hours. The blood-engorged larvae develop into $^3/8$" dark brown cigar-shaped puparia from which the adult blowflies emerge after ten to fourteen days to fly to another cavity and repeat the cycle. Puparia found in the nest after the young have fledged should be destroyed as the nest is removed.

If only a few larvae (ten or less) are found when checking the nestlings, lifting up the nest and gently shaking it will dislodge most of them and they can be brushed out. Alternatively, a new nest may be constructed of clean dry grass .

Bluebirds sometimes use pine needles and may fly some distance from the nestbox to obtain the needles even when grass is readily available. Blowfly larvae have not been found in pine needle nests. Some trail monitors slip pine needles under grass nests. Indications are that this will help prevent blowfly infestations.

A 1" deep false floor of $^3/8$" hardware cloth, has been used, based on the theory that the larvae drop through and are unable to crawl back up (Campbell, 1980, 1982). However, these elevated subfloors do not always stop the larvae from crawling back up into the nest, though the pupae do drop through (Bacon, 1989). Moreover, both bluebirds and tree swallows tended to avoid the nest boxes with false floors. The fake floor should not be used in shallow boxes if this would raise the nest dangerously high. The feet of bluebird and tree swallow nestlings have been caught in the hardware cloth inserts.

If the infestation is serious (fifty or more larvae), a natural insecticide, pyrethrin, will not only kill the larvae but will repel the adult blowfly. Tested extensively on canaries, the insecticide sprayed under the nest and even directly around the nestlings (but not into the eyes) apparently has no immediate or residual effect on birds. Birds and mammals can break down pyrethroids and pass them through their bodies rapidly. Flys Away II®, which contains .10% pyrethrin, is made by the Farnam Company for horse wounds and is sold in horse supply stores. It has proven very effective.

Jerry Eastman, of Rochester, Minnesota, found a roll-on version of Flys Away II. It is viscous. He saturates cotton balls with it and slips them under the nest whenever blowflies or blackflies are really bothersome. His method extends the effectiveness of the chemical. Julie Hineman, LaValle, Wisconsin used Eastman's idea, puts wood shavings between the saturated cotton and the bottom of the nest. A spray for dogs, Spectro-D, by Pitman-Moore, has .05% pyrethrin when diluted as directed. Two products made specifically for caged pet birds have .10% and .03% pyrethrin respectively: Hills Bird and Cage Spray and 8-in-1 Mite and Lice Bird Spray.

The sprays listed have been used by bluebirders. They contain only pyrethrin and the necessary propellants, but even these relatively benign chemicals have precautionary labels which warn of environmental and human hazards and should be used with care. They break down rapidly, thus their effect is short-lived.

These pesticides should by used only when absolutely necessary, when insect infestations are so serious as to threaten death to the nestlings, and in no stronger concentration than is needed to be effective (.10%). While pyrethrin has been tested for residual effects when sprayed around small birds, the effects of their eating insects killed by chemicals have not been so thoroughly investigated. It is always better to change to a clean nest if possible.

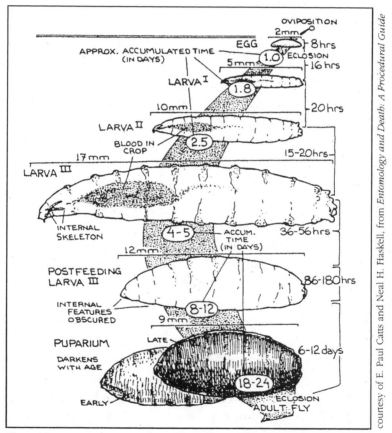

The evidence grows: size timeline of hypothetical immature blow fly development

145

One of the unfortunate side effects of using pyrethrin or any other insecticide in nestboxes which contain blowfly larvae is that it also will kill a small wasp (*Nasonia vitripennis*) which parasitizes the blowfly larvae. The tiny (3 mm) wasp, sometimes called a jewel wasp because of its brilliant iridescent metallic color, drills into the pupa, paralyzes it, and lays eggs on the surface of the developing fly. The pupal wasps then emerge from the blowfly pupal case and the cycle repeats. Blowflies leave the nestbox to overwinter in leaf litter or other protected areas, but their parasitized pupae left in the nestbox has, in laboratory conditions simulating winter and then spring, produced a new generation of *Nasonia.* (Darling and Thompson-Delaney, 1992). These wasp parasites will also overwinter if nest with the blowfly pupae if tossed into the leaf litter in woods, and will emerge in late spring. To be sure only the beneficial wasp emerges, store the old nest in a bucket in a dry environment like a garage, and cover the bucket with $^1/8$" screen. Only the wasp will be able to emerge in the spring.

Gnats and **blackflies** can congregate in masses in and around the nest box, biting the nestlings as wll as attacking the monitor. Although they breed in running water, the infestations of blackflies seem to be particularly severe near wide areas of marshy land. Pyrethrin is effective with these small flies but must be repeated every two or three days if used as a preventative.

Lice (*Mallophaga*) and mites (*Acarina*) are not often found on bluebirds. Don't be fooled by piles of small greyish flecks under a used bluebird nest. These are most likely the skin scales left when the pin feathers erupted. Rarely are lice a serious problem, though they may be carried in with chicken feathers used by tree swallows and house sparrows. Fleas and wormsare rarely found. Pyrethrin is effective on mites, lice, and fleas. The small tick which carries Lyme disease has been found on some migrating ground-foraging birds, but not on bluebirds.

Ants swarming over unfeathered nestlings can cause death. In the south fire ants are a problem, especially during times of continual rain when they are forced out of their ground mounds. Fire ants have prevented adults from entering the nestbox and have killed nestlings. (On the flip side, they have also carried off blowfly larvae! (Sims, 1988). Ant poison such as Terro® can be used, either by slipping a piece of saturated paper or a bottle cap filled with the poison under the nest or by stapling soaked Q-tips® under the box. One person has stopped fire ants by wrapping the pole with duct tape <u>inside out</u> so the ants got caught in the sticky side. The procedure will have to be repeated.

Pyrethrin spray is also effective against ants. A wide ring of Tree Tanglefoot® or heavy grease regularly applied around the post prevents ants from climbing, but fire ants may collect so thickly on the grease that the oncoming hordes just walk right over the bodies stuck in the grease. According to Keith Kridler (1999) fire ants are drawn to electro-magnetic fields, and their populations will be ten times greater within a 200-300 yard wide path under major transmission lines than outside that area.

Paper wasps will attach their nests inside the roof of a nestbox or underthe floor and attack the *bluebirder.* Bluebirds will not construct a nest in a box containing wasps. Pyrethrin can be sprayed into an empty box at night. Plug the holes until morning. Soft bar soap, petroleum jelly, or grease will prevent attachment of the paper nest.

Large dead **beetles** found in vacated nest boxes sometimes puzzle bluebirders. Possible origins are:
(1) They were brought in by parent bluebirds and were either rejected by the nestlings or lost in the nesting material;
(2) Carrion beetles (Family *Silphidae*) have been attracted to decaying material in the nest box; or
(3) Burying beetles (*Nicrophorus marginatus*) have been at-

tracted in the same way. Sometimes the black carrion beetle (which has bright orange or reddish markings) is found with dead nestlings. It was not the cause of death, but came afterward to feed on carcasses. The burying beetle ($^3/4$ - $1^1/8$", shiny black with two stippled orange bands) feeds on fly larvae and dead small birds (Peterson, 1989).

Earwigs can get into a bluebird box. Usually only a few are present, but Ed Bailey of Michigan had one nest so thick with earwigs that it was actually moving! Replacing with a clean nest <u>dry</u> is one answer — earwigs like moist conditions. Grease on the post should stop further infiltration. Dick Tuttle of Ohio reports that a teaspoon of coffee grounds sprinkled in the bottom of a box would discourage earwigs. Earwigs like damp places to hide. They are most active at night (Bower 1998).

Pesticides

At this time, no other pesticide beside pyrethrin can be recommended for use in bluebird boxes. Sad tales continue to come in each year. Sometimes it is the misuse of supposedly safe chemicals. After a tragic die-off of tree swallows in Aitkin County, Minnesota, detective work by Bill Samuelson, Dick Peterson, and John Thompson determined that the simple miscalculation in concentration of roadside spray was responsible. The applicators failed to dilute it!

The chemicals *BTI®* and *Altosid®*, mosquito larvicides supposedly safe for the environment, slow development and weaken ducklings. Research funded by BBRP (1991), revealed the development of tree swallow young on BTI-treated marshland was also retarded, though the nestlings did fledge eventually, apparently healthy. Bluebirds also eat dragonflies and mayflies which feed on larval mosquitoes. BTI has also been used in aerial sprays for cankerworm, another bluebird food.

Diazinon® does not eliminate parasites from nests; its proven mortality to birds has resulted in the EPA outlawing its use on golf courses and sod farms. The residual effects of Roundup® and Rodeo® have not been studied. Roundup is supposed to be safe, yet tree swallow nestlings died recently in New York state in nestboxes around which Roundup had been sprayed. No other discernible cause could be discovered (Cook, 1998). All three, Diazinon, Roundup and Rodeo, are extremely toxic in water. "Water-soluble" on the label is a warning in itself of how easily the toxic effects can dissipate. Handling precautions for humans should be a warning as well. Diazinon is a broad spectrum nematode. When lawns are treated for grub control, dead birds are a likely result (Thomas, 1999).

Shell strips have been used in nest boxes, but the chlorinated hydrocarbon Vapone, in even a small half-inch piece of the strip, is toxic to birds. There is a long-term residual effect on young bluebird fledglings after they have left the nest and the effect may even carry through *their* eggs after they mature.

Carbaryl (Sevin®), safe in mild doses (such as a 5% dry dust), has been tested on canaries and chickens with — so far —no noticeable toxic results. It is toxic in sufficient concentration. It will kill bees and is toxic to pregnant mammals. Its use in vegetable gardens is strongly suspected in nestling deaths (Krueger, 1988).

Powdered sulfur even in light concentrations has killed martins that ingested it when it accumulated into heaps. It does not deteriorate nor lose its effectiveness. Diatomaceous earth (DE) has been recommended for use in martin houses. One must be very careful that it is loosely sprinkled and does not clump or get ingested, (where it would work just like ground glass!)

Rotenone, a natural product like pyrethrin, breaks down rapidly, but is moderately toxic to warm-blooded animals. Excessive amounts have killed baby chickens. Research testing the ability

149

of Rotenone to kill blowflies showed little value, but was extremely efficient at killing the jewel wasp which helps control blowflies (Berner, 1999). Malathion, which deteriorates rapidly, has not been tested enough on birds.

Fumes from naphthalene (mothballs) has been fatal to canary eggs and chicks. Any bluebirder who tries naphthalene around the bottom of nestbox posts to attempt to throw raccoons off scent should be very sure the flakes or balls are in a container that can't be opened by young humans or animals.

None of these pesticides should be used in bluebird nestboxes.

Do not put nest boxes where lawn care companies are employed unless you have checked to find out the chemicals being used. Large companies with extensive lawns, and managers of golf courses and cemeteries are usually more concerned with weed-free, uniform greens than with possible effects on wildlife. More research is needed, but songbirds, notably ground feeders like robins and bluebirds, have died within a few hours after commercial lawn applications have been used. Similar precautions should be followed if individuals treat their own lawns.

Farm fields are subject to pesticide spraying. Corn-borer larvae and moths, alfalfa beetles, and grasshoppers are favorite foods of bluebirds. Where spraying can be anticipated, nestboxes less than one mile away should be closed.

Vandalism is discussed in Chapter 4.

Yet another problem is the open deep cavity NOT intended to attract bluebirds: chimneys, goal posts, TreeTubes®, new posts for PVC horse fencing. All these open-topped temptations can mean death for bluebirds and many other songbirds. Such openings should be screened or capped.

Summary of Bluebird Predators and Problems
Clues and Perpetrators

1. Nest

Clue: Little sticks in box, often up to top, maybe over bluebird nest: *House wren.*

Clue: Feathers (usually white) on top of bluebird nest: *Tree swallow.**

Clue: Debris, paper, weeds along with grass nest, often circled high over hole: *House sparrow (English sparrow).*

Clue: Shredded bark, leaves, etc., filling box: *Red squirrel.*

Clue: Shredded milkweed, seeds, coneflower seed heads: *Mice.*

Clue: Coarse grass mixed with green weeds. Eggs robin-size but lighter blue: *Starling.*

*Note: Nests of tree swallows, nests lined with moss and fur (Chickadee); large grass with bits of shed snakeskin (Crested flycatcher); shreds of inner bark, fur, feathers, hair (Nuthatch); should be welcome if there are boxes enough.

2. **Eggs**

Clue: Bluebird eggs suddenly disappear, nest undisturbed: *House wren, house sparrow, snake.*
Clue: Bluebird eggs disappear, nest partially pulled out of hole: *Raccoon,, cat.*
Clue: Bluebird eggs shattered on ground or in nest: *House wren, house sparrow, red squirrel, chipmunk.*
Clue: Tiny holes pecked in eggs: *House wren.*

3. **Nestlings**

Clue: Nestlings gone, nest intact, parents still around: *Cat, snake, wren house sparrow.*
Clue: Nestlings gone, nest partially pulled through hole. Grass below may be trampled, feathers around: *Raccoon, cat.*
Clue: Nestlings dead outside box, perhaps one per day: *House wren, house sparrow.*
Clue: Nestlings suddenly dead in box, with bodies unmarked, stomachs full, parents still around: *Pesticide poisoning.*
Clue: Young nestlings dead in wet nest: *Hypothermia.*
Clue: Nestlings dead in nest, emaciated: *Predator got both parents.*
Clue: Nestling dead in nest, little blackflies around, red welts on bodies, especially under wings: *Gnat.*
Clue: Nestlings dead in nest, large red welts over bodies, black pupae or gray maggots under nest: *Blowfly larvae.*
Clue: Nestlings mutilated in nest: *House sparrow, or mice, red squirrel.*
Clue: Female dead in box, head feathers and/or eyes pecked out: *House sparrow.*

Perpetrators and solutions

Ants. Slip a paste or liquid ant poison under nest, where it will not be reached by young or adults. Or staple a Q-tip soaked in liquid ant poison under nest or bottom of house. Apply a band of grease around post. Make a ring of TangleFoot® or grease around the post or pole.

Blowfly. If small black cigar-shaped pupae or gray maggots are found near bottom of nest, lift nest with young out and shake out as many pupae and larvae as possible. Brush off floor. If nest is wet and highly infested, construct a new one of dry grass. Check nestlings for attached larvae and replace them in nest.

Cats. Usually leave some feathers around. If cat is known and cannot be confined during nesting period, front claws should be trimmed to prevent it from snaring young from box and adults who are dive-bombing it. Trimmed and declawed cats can still climb. Use cat/coon guards on box. Itinerant cats should be disposed of. Cat/coon guards on box will not stop cat from getting adult birds on ground.

English (house) sparrow—the worst avian enemy of bluebirds! Try all methods to eliminate. Be sure to get male sparrow if possible; destroy eggs and nests.

Gnats or **blackflies** (tiny). Use pyrethrin> spray for heavy swarms and infestation of nestlings.

House wren. Keep sticks removed. Move bluebird boxes 200-300 feet away from trees or brush.

Hypothermia. Check nest boxes after heavy, slanting rains. Replace wet nest with new dry grass. Young nestlings may die if left in wet nest. Dampness also attracts blowflies.

Mice. Often nest over winter in closed boxes. Leave boxes open during winter if they become a problem. Continue to throw out, but use care not to breathe in dust from nests. Use climb-proof mounting post.

Pesticide poisoning. More often a problem at second nesting only. Try to determine if poisons will be used nearby by farmer, groundskeeper, gardener, lawn-care company; close boxes to prevent use.

Raccoon. Use separate smooth metal posts, or smoothly wrapped tin on wood posts; try cone guards on post, cat/coon guards on box. Avoid fencelines.

Red squirrel. Keep nest boxes sealed in winter, or leave open. Climb-proof posts as above, and keep away from trees and from which saplings squirrels could leap.

Starling. Use starling trap. Eliminate. Be sure box entrance hole is minimum size for bluebirds.

Snake. Climb-proof separate posts or heavily grease.

Tree or violet-green swallow. Pair boxes 10-25 feet apart. Remove used bluebird nests promptly for maximum nesting opportunities.

Notes

Notes

Chapter 8

Food

Plantings

The eastern, mountain and western bluebirds which migrate away in the winter from their breeding areas are seeking good foraging areas as well as nesting sites when they return. All three are insectivorous — mainly insect eaters. However, in planning our gardens and landscaping for wildlife, we can include plants whose fruit may be used by bluebirds upon early spring arrival, in natural supplements for their nestlings, or in late fall as they prepare to migrate. Two percent of the adult diet all year round is wild fruit. From October to February, during migration and while on wintering grounds, one-third or more of their diet may be wild fruit. More and different varieties will be utilized by bluebirds in areas where bluebirds stay over the winter.

We can also experiment by picking and freezing some fruits (especially berries) to offer in feed trays in times of stress. Try holly berries, mistletoe berries, multiflora and wild rose hips. (The last should not be cultivated, and care should be taken to not propagate them further. They may invade and damage native plant communities.) The best policy is to plant only those beneficial species that are native to your area. That way you will help avoid the kind of usurpation among plants by invasive non-native flora that has occurred with such devastating effects among bluebirds by invasive non-native avians. While restoring ecological conditions for bluebirds, you will be preserving the habitat for other species. Bluebirds eat some berries, like poison ivy and poison oak, we wouldn't dream of propagating,

Carrol Henderson's book, *Landscaping for Wildlife* (1988), is an excellent guide for Northerners. Some of the beneficial plants listed below are native to, and hardy in the zones 3, 4, and 5. Check with a local nursery or with the USDA Plant Hardiness Zone Map (Miscellaneous Publication 1475) to determine what growing zone you are in, then select plants that are hardy in your specific zone. These plants are only suggestions, used successfully by at least one bluebirder. Many other birds will certainly benefit as well.

Common Name	Botanical Name
Smooth serviceberry	*Amelanchier laevis*
Juneberry or Shadbush	*Amelanchier alnifolia*
Chokeberry	*Aronia melanocarpa*
Bittersweet	*Celastrus scandens*
Common hackberry	*Celtis occidentalis*
Red osier dogwood	*Cornus stolonifera*
Cotoneaster *	*Cotoneaster divaricata*
Hawthorn	*Crataegus spp.*
Bush honeysuckle	*Diervilla lonicer*
Russian olive**	*Elaeagnus angustifolia*
Autumn olive**	*Elaeagnus umbellata*
Burning bush*	*Euonymous alatus*
Black huckleberry	*Gaylussacia brachycera*
Winterberry	*Ilex verticillata*
Eastern red cedar	*Juniperus virginiana*
Amur honeysuckle *	*Lonicera maackii*
Tartarian honeysuckle **	*Lonicera tartarica*
Flowering crabapple	*Malus spp*
Red Mulberry	*Morus rubra*
Sweet gale	*Myrica gale*
Virginia creeper	*Parthenocissus quinquefolia*

Amur bird cherry*	*Prunus maakii*
Pin cherry	*Prunus pennsylvanica*
Black cherry	*Prunus serotina*
Chokecherry	*Prunus virginiana*
Firethorn*	*Pyracantha coccinea*
Common buckthorn**	*Rhamnus catharticus*
Smooth sumac	*Rhus glabra*
Poison ivy	*Rhus radicans*
Staghorn sumac	*Rhus typhina*
Multiflora rose***	*Rosa multiflora*
Raspberry/blackberry	*Rubus spp.*
American elderberry	*Sambucus canadensis*
Scarlet elderberry	*Sambucus pubens*
American mountain ash	*Sorbus americana*
Showy mountain ash	*Sorbus decora*
Arrowwood	*Viburnum dentatum*
Nannyberry	*Viburnum lentago*
Downy arrowwood	*Viburnum rafinesquianum*
Highbush cranberry	*Viburnum trilobum*
Wild grape	*Vitis spp.*

* This plant is an introduced species
** This plant is not native and will tend to invade wild plant communities, displacing native species and disrupting natural habitats. May be illegal in some areas.
*** Be careful—though one of the best for bluebirds, it's a pernicious spreader and planting it is illegal in some areas.

Western bluebird diet includes mistletoe, toyon berries (*Heteromeles arbutifolia*), firethorn, privet (*ligustrum eleacease*), lantana (*verbenaceae montevidensis*) and carrotwood (*cupaniopsis anacardioides*). The skin of the carrotwood seed is what is digested; they then regurgitated the seed itself. (Purvis, 1999).

Veteran bluebirder Jack Finch of Bailey, North Carolina, is able to keep flowering dogwood (*Cornus Florida*) berries for extended periods. The berries are a favorite fruit of eastern bluebirds wintering in the south. In mid-October or early November he visits 15 to 30 year old trees, when the berries are ripe but before the leaves fall (and thus before others birds pick the berries clean). With permission from the property owners, he carefully picks (not shakes) berries, getting from 5 to 25 pounds in a good year from a single mature tree. He cleans them, sorting out any damaged, dark or wormy berries. They are then stored in small ventilated, unsealed containers at 29-32°F The temperature is very important, and should be regularly checked. Berries are checked every 10-12 days and bad, dark or moldy berries removed (and thrown out under bushes for immediate feeding.

Jack also has kept a few berries in sawdust mix, just below freezing, for over six months." Berries mixed with equal parts by volume of dry wood sawdust or fine shavings keep well in storage, maintain quality, and last longer than any method... Berries layered with paper towels in plastic buckets keep well also". Training the bluebirds to eat the berries must be done early before severe weather begins. Start with placing the berries in flat open trays easily visible to the bluebirds. Then gradually the feeding place can be moved to a covered place before the snow flies.

Insects will always be the preferred bluebird food, but the berries can sustain them in during bad weather, and in North Carolina the birds have continued to consume dogwood berries even through the first brood (Finch, 1994).

Supplemental Offerings and Emergency Food

Another good topic of debate among bluebirders is whether bluebirds should be offered food in the fall. In times of stress—

early in spring or when parent birds are having trouble finding sufficient food for their nestlings — frozen fruit of the plants listed can be offered. In addition, try mealworms, sunflower hearts, peanut hearts (chopped), small bits of canned dog food, suet, softened chopped raisins or currants, small chopped *unsalted* nut meats, hard-boiled egg yolk, and corn bread. Howard Malone, of Marion, Mississippi, substitutes cottonseed meal, which is 42% protein, for chopped nuts. Different circumstances and the amount of stress determines whether the adult bluebirds will accept your offerings.

Hamburger or ground meat is not as easily digested as canned dog food. Some bluebirders use lard and peanut hearts or shaved suet and peanut hearts. Others use crushed birdseed with peanut butter and bacon grease, but peanut butter should be used only as a binding agent; alone it could choke birds. Bacon grease is salty; fresh water should be readily available.

Just before and during the nesting season, crushed egg shells, rich in calcium carbonate, will benefit not only blue-birds, but other birds as well, including barn swallows, violet-green and tree swallows, flycatchers, kingbirds, robins, orioles, flickers, purple martins, and, later in the season, goldfinches. Without enough calcium, a laying female will have thinner-shelled eggs, a smaller clutch, and slowed hatching rate. Fast-food restaurants, hospitals, nursing homes, and bakeries are sources of egg shells.

Raking, watering, and turning over heavily compacted soil will make it easier for bluebirds to find ground insects. Finding grasshoppers, crickets, and ground beetles when the nestlings are eight days or more, and placing them, along with mealworm beetles, on a nearby stump or temporary feeder in plain sight of parent bluebirds may do more to set up a good opportunity for photography than to provide a continuous dietary supplement. Before the nestlings are six days old, try softer grubs, larvae,

161

mealworms and cutworms. Small earthworms can be offered, but only in moderation. Do not put any food directly into the nest box. The parent birds will prepare the food you have offered by mashing the worms, decapitating the mealworms, and so forth. They also know instinctively which insects or grubs the fledglings should not have. Do not feed sowbugs or pillbugs—they could be intermediate hosts for parasites.

You may be surprised, as some birdwatchers have been, by seeing bluebirds actually come to a regular bird feeder containing sunflower chips or hearts. This may happen in early spring or with an erratic bluebird who somehow failed to get the "go south" message, has perhaps fed on wild berries late into the fall, and then finds the protein in sunflower hearts the only available fare. Sunflower hearts may be a second choice when all the dogwood berries, sumac, etc. have been consumed. In the southern states, bluebirds regularly eat sunflower hearts over the whole winter, supplemented by other food, and are known to bring their fledglings to the feeder later on.

Many bluebirders raise mealworms to keep on hand for regular offerings and for emergency feeding of bluebirds as well as other species. Most feeder birds except goldfinches will eat them. Mealworms are available in most pet and bait stores, and by telephone order from producers who specialize in bulk quantities of them. They are not really worms at all, they are the larval stages of the beetle *Tenebrio Molitor*. It's easy to keep a colony going. They multiply rapidly and may be kept in the refrigerator, becoming active when warmed up. (See Appendix for tips on raising mealworms, and for suppliers.)

Adding dry dog food to the mealworms' food mixture a few days before offering them to bluebirds, will supply extra protein. Dry feline food contains even more protein.

Will bluebirds become dependent on your handout? No! But supplying mealworms in times of trouble has definitely at times made the difference in how healthy the nestlings are and whether they survive to fledging. Parent bluebirds, by instinct , will not stop eating in order to save the nestlings. If insect food is scarce, the young will die first. If the parents survive, they can breed again. During nesting time, just one pair of bluebirds can dispense with 80 mealworms a day, twice that if no other food is available. The mealworms can be supplemented with berries and nutritionally balanced made-to-order recipes, like Bluebird Banquet.

Linda Janilla, of Stillwater, MN, was awarded a Bluebird Recovery Program Research Grant to study bluebird nutritional requirements and produce an artificial, completely balanced bluebird food recipe. Her *Bluebird Banquet* has sustained blue-birds overwintering in many areas, and has been heartily en-dorsed by adult and fledgling bluebirds. "For successful feeding of bluebirds, the birds must be educated or conditioned. The best time to begin a feeding program would be spring, when the birds first return and natural foods are scarce. It is a time when insects are not fully active and berries are few."

While bluebirds are most receptive to an open tray or dish as a feeder, so are undesirable birds, and the food is exposed to rain. You can start with a small open container near a nestbox, then   gradually train them to an enclosed, glass-sided feeder, with $1^1/2$" holes at either end. They can be "trained" by gradually moving the open dish, to which they have become accustomed ,toward the feeder. A few meal worms placed on top of the open dish and on the feeder will encourage "sampling." They may be reluctant to enter the feeder; one or both of the glass slides can be removed until they are used to it. Putting strips of tape horizontally across the glass will lessen chances of the birds, once inside, trying to fly out through the glass and getting panicked. Five to ten days of "training" may be necessary, and should be observed carefully, as occasionally bluebirds inside the feeder will become confused by the glass. Be sure to keep the feeder clean.

Linda's *Bluebird Banquet*: 1 cup peanut butter, 4 cups yellow cornmeal; 1 cup rendered suet, melted; 1 cup flour; 1 cup zante' raisins (small raisins); 1 cup small sunflower chips, 1 cup peanut hearts. (If organic cornmeal is used, omit flour.)

Out on the trail, small plastic shallow cups or tuna or cat cans can be attached near the nestbox for mealworms, waxworms, or the *Bluebird Banquet*, if the bluebirds are accustomed to that. Bluebirds will soon become familiar with a cache of mealworms that you bring for them and put just in a crevice in a high rock or a nearby stump. Do not leave more than a few mealworms out - other birds, and potential predators may be attracted as well.

Continuing to supply mealworms at feeders in the fall, when bluebirds should migrate, will not persuade them to try and winter over . It could make them linger a day or two more. If they then are stopped by snow, you should continue feeding a few more days until they can leave.

Feeding Orphaned Nestlings and Fledglings

Chapter 5 – Monitoring, offered suggestions on how to determine if nestlings are really "orphaned." Switching and fostering out to other nest boxes where nestlings will be adopted is *always preferable* to trying to hand raise them. Of course, care must be taken to not overload the foster parents.

Not only is hand-raising rarely successful, but as stressed earlier, *a special permit is required*. Without a permit, you will have to find a licensed rehabilitator or another bluebirder who has a permit and can legally care for them. Once you are sure

Mountain
bluebird
female
- Yellowstone
National Park

Charles Sleicher

Jim & Ann Auer

All bluebirds love to play in water

PLATE *33*

Eastern
bluebird
male

Lois Nissen

John Thompson

Mealworms attract male eastern bluebird

PLATE 34

James R. Gallagher - Sea & Sage Audubon

Male western bluebird

Myrna Pearmar

Male mountain bluebird

PLATE *35*

Donna Hagerman

Female mountain bluebird

Mryna Pearman

Young mountain bluebirds in box

PLATE 36

neither parent has returned to the nestbox over a four-hour period, the nestlings should be kept warm and transported in a covered shoe box or other small dark container lined with <u>smooth</u> toweling.

If there will be a time delay and the nestlings are already obviously stressed, canned dog food mashed into small bits, either alone or mixed 50/50 with hard-boiled egg, can be offered with a soft applicator or dull tweezers. Force feeding may be necessary the first few times, by means of the blunt end of a toothpick well back in the mouth, behind the tongue.   An alternative to try: liver, egg, and meat-based baby food. Science Diet®—feline maintenance dry pellets soaked in water — is an excellent high protein diet also containing calcium and phosphorus. Mealworms (with the heads removed for young nestlings) and "softened" earthworm pieces can be tried.

Frances Hanes (1984), who did have the necessary permit, had success in raising nestlings by moistening dry mynah bird food (a fruit-based diet for insectivores) with warm water until it felt crumbly, mixing it with small amounts of Cycle I® dog food, then feeding it in tiny bits.

Water should be used only as a moistening agent, never forced alone.   If the nestlings seem particularly stressed, Gatorade® should be used as the moistening agent. If long-term feeding is anticipated, a vitamin supplement such as that used for canaries should be included. Natural food should be offered as often as possible. Older nestlings — two weeks or more — will eat grasshoppers, beetles, caterpillars, spiders, and moths. Crickets are available from most pet stores. Nestlings should be fed every twenty minutes at least, from dawn to dark.

Removing fecal sacs will keep the area clean. Lining a nest-shaped box with Kleenex® or tissues will permit frequent changing. A slightly warm heating pad under the box should be used for young nestlings. Take care that the interior of the box does not exceed 100 F°— heating pads can easily overheat. The birds should be kept out of drafts as well.

Again, it should be stressed that—as sure as we may be that we can take good care — fostering out nestlings to natural parents is far better for the nestlings. Even if they do survive, they will quickly become imprinted to their human care-provider and the likelihood of their survival once returned to the wild will be very low. In fostering out nestlings to other active bluebird nestboxes, be careful to match ages of nestlings, and to not overburden the feeding parents. Here again, a convenient mealworm supply will help the adults feed their extended family.

The nestling left behind when its siblings fledge presents a different picture, as it cannot be placed elsewhere. A bluebirder who checks and observes the nest boxes frequently may be lucky enough to discover the abandoned young before it expires. Again, a permit is needed to care for it, and it too may become imprinted. It should be fed every half hour from seven in the morning to eleven at night, but kept in a bird cage or something more open than a shoe box, and the cage should have perches and a water container. Food could include the natural larger insects and mealworms, hard-boiled egg yolk, scraped dog biscuit, and dibasic calcium phosphate with Vitamin D (Price, 1982). Bluebirder and licensed rehabilitator Darrell Stave of Baxter, Minnesota, uses pieces of mealworms and Hill's Prescription Diet Feline c/d® cat food (Stave (1998). Opportunities to try long flights should be offered frequently and it should be released near other bluebirds as soon as it eats natural food well by itself and can fly some distance. When released near other recent fledglings, it may be adopted by the bluebird parents.

166

Check out the possibility of putting the caged orphan outside where the adult bluebird can find it. The attitude of the adults will determine its chances for adoption.

Notes

Appendix

Organizations—Membership and Items for Sale

The North American Bluebird Society
P.O. Box 74
Darlington, WI   e-mail: nabluebird@aol.com
           Web page: www.cobleskill.edu/nabs/
  Membership: Annual dues—Students and seniors $10.00,
Regular $15.00; 3-year Regular $42 [Other categories]
   Includes quarterly issue of *Bluebird* newsletter
   Annual and regional meetings.
   Nestbox and other information; Nestbox Approvals; Transcontinen
     tal Bluebird Trail
   Sale items: Catalog of nest boxes, patches,decals, bluebird tapes,
     stationery, books, etc.
   Slide program rental.

The Bluebird Recovery Program of Minnesota (BBRP)
Audubon Chapter of Minneapolis
P.O. Box 3801
Minneapolis, MN 55403   e-mail; scrivoo1@tc.umn.edu
   Suggested annual donation (tax-deductible) of $8.00. $15/2 years,
etc. Membership packet includes full-scale Peterson plan, Gilbertson
PVC plan, Noel guard plan, brochure, quarterly newsletter, predator and
problem guide, nesting chart.
   A directory of U.S.bluebirders reporting to BBRP, bluebird report
form.
   Annual conference third Saturday in April. Workshops.
   Sale items: clothing, bluebird tapes, books, art items, stationery, etc.

The following organizations are affiliates of the North American Bluebird Society, and have various offerings. Please check with individual organizations.

Source: **http: //www.cobleskill.edu/nabs/affiliate.htm**

CANADA

Alberta
Calgary Area Bluebird Trail
    Monitors
c/o Don Stiles
20 Lake Wapta Rise SE
Calgary, Alberta T2J 2M9

Ellis Bird Farm, Ltd.
Box 5090
Lacombe, Alberta T4L 1W7
http://www.wep.ab.ca/ellisbirdfarm
Contact: Myrna Pearman

Mountain Bluebird Trails Society
1725 Lakeside Road South
Lethbridge, Alberta T1K 3G9
Contact: Bob Harrison
403-328-0863

British Columbia
Southern Interior Bluebird Trail
Society
Sherry Linn, Vice-President
Box 494, Oliver, B.C. VOH 1TO
e mail: goldstrm@vip.net

Manitoba
The Friends of the Bluebirds
3011 Park Ave
Brandon, Manitoba R7B 2K3
e mail: smitha@brandon.ca

Ontario
Ontario Eastern Bluebird Society
2-165 Green Valley Drive
Kitchener, Ontario N2P 1K3
Contact: Bill Read

UNITED STATES

Arkansas
Bella Vista Bluebird Society
c/o Jim Janssen, President
27 Britten Circle
Belle Vista, AR 72714

California
California Bluebird Recovery Program
2021 Ptarmigan Drive #1
Walnut Creek, CA 94595
e-mail: cbrp@value.net.

Colorado
The Bluebird Project
The Denver Audubon Society &
The Colroado Division of Wildlife
6060 Broadway
Denver, CO 80216
Tel: 303-291-9253
e mail: bluebird53@juno.com

Georgia
Bluebirds Over Georgia
5858 Silver Ridge Rd
Stone Mountain, GA 30087
e mail: fgsawyer@mindspring.com

Illinois
Illinois Bluebird Recovery Program
15 Cedar Rim Trail
Galena, IL 61036
contact: Grace Storch

APPENDIX

Indiana
Indiana Bluebird Society
P.O. Box 356
Leesburg, IN 46538
e mail: bluebird11@juno.com

The Brown County Bluebird Society
c/o Dan Sparks.
Box 660
Nashville, IN 47448

Iowa
Johnson County Songbird Project
2511 Highway 1 SW
Iowa City, IA 52240

Maine
Bluebird Association of Maine
c/o Lisa Paige
RFD 4, Box 7600
Gardiner, ME 04345

Minnesota
Bluebird Recovery Program
Audubon Chapter of Minneapolis
P.O. Box 3801
Minneapolis, MN 55403
e mail: scriv001@tc.umn.edu

Montana
Mountain Bluebird Trails
P.O. Box 794
Ronan, MT 59864
Contact: Bob Niebuhr
e mail: blubrdbob@prodigy.net

Nebraska
Bluebirds Across Nebraska
c/o Steve Eno
Box 67157
Lincoln, NE 68506
e mail: cleno@aol.com

New York
New York Bluebird Society
15 Birdle Lane
Dryden, NY 13053
e mail: jrfk2@ibm.net

Schoharie County Bluebird Society
c/o Kevin Berner
SUNY Cobleskill
Cobleskill NY 12043

North Carolina
North Carolina Bluebird Society
P.O. Box 4191
Greensboro, NC 27404

Rutherford County Bluebird Club
P.O. Box 247
Ellenboro, NC 28040Contact;
Christopher Greene

Ohio
Ohio Bluebird Society
c/o Doug LeVasseur
20680 Township Road #120
Senecaville, OH 43780
e mail: emdlev@clover.net
www.obsbluebirds.com

Oklahoma
Oklahoma Bluebird Society
c/o Norma Streator
Rt. 2, Tailor's Ferry Area North
Wagoner, PK 74467
614-785-5220

Oregon
Prescott Western Bluebird Recovery
c/o Patricia Johnston   Project
7717 SW 50th
Portland, OR 97219

171

Oregon
Audubon Society of Corvallis
P.O. Box 148
Corvallis, OR 97339
Contact: Elsie Eltzroth

Pennsylvania
Bluebird Society of Pennsylvania
P.O. Box 267
Enola, PA 17035-0267
e mail: bsporg@aol.com
Tel: 717-938-4089 (Kathy Clark, Pres.)
   717-651-0580 (Diane Barbin, Sec.)

Virginia
The Virginia Bleubird Society
c/o Julie Kitruff/Anne Little
3403 Carly Lane
Woodbridge, VA 22129

Washington
Cascadia Bluebird and
      Purple Martin Society
Dr. Michael Pietro
1537 Lakeway Place
Bellingham, WA 98226

Wisconsin
Bluebird Restoration Association
   of Wisconsin
Rt. 1, Box 137 Akron Ave
Plainfield, WI 54966

Lafayette County Bluebird Society
14953 Hwy 23
Darlington, WI 53530

Sources of Nestboxes, Kits, and Accessories

The North American Bluebird Society, The Bluebird Recovery Program of Minnesota, and many of the affiliates listed above have sources of nestboxes, kits and accessories. (So do many nature catalogues, but be sure to verify authentic and recommended designs.)

Steve Gilbertson
HC 5, Box 31
Aitkin, MN 56431.
Tel: 218-927-1953.
   Birch-print PVC box. $8 each (minimum order $2 for $16 including postage.
   Gilwood nestbox $8 each, minimum order 2/$16 including postage.
   Universal sparrow trap $6 including shipping

Sources of Nest Boxes, Kits, Accessories

Ahlgren Construction Company
12989 Otchipwe Avenue North
Stillwater, MN 55082
Fax: 651-351-9586

(These are 1999 prices—write for current price list. Cedar
and siding construction.)
Peterson Bluebird Box kit. 3/4" solid cedar with hardboard
sides. $8 plus $5 S&P for first kit, $2 S&P for each addi-
tional.
Peterson Bluebird Box fully assembled. $10 plus $5 S&P
first box, $2 additional.
Wire Noel Cat/Coon Guard $1.50 plus $4 S& P for 1-10
guards
Wire Noel Guard with Adapter for Peterson box. $2.50. $4
S&P for 1 - 10 guards

John Holm
2014 Avenue G
Gothenburg, NE 69138
308-537-2323

Rectangular cedar box assembled with wooden predator
guard, $5.00 postpaid.
Rectangular cedar box assembled with wooden predator
guard, $6.50 postpaid.
Peterson box kit with Noel guard, cedar/pine/masonite,
$9.50 plus shipping.
1 $^{3}/_{16}$"wooden slot box. Kit, $4.50 plus shipping.
Slot box assembled, $6.60 plus shipping.

In-box Sparrow Traps

Universal Sparrow Trap: See page 135

Bauldry Sparrow Trap

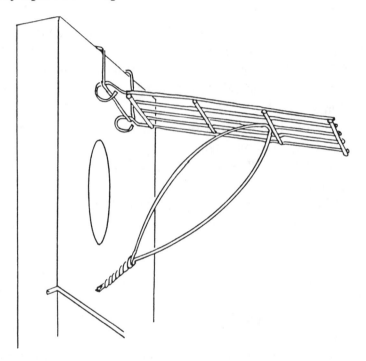

The Vince Bauldry bird trap uses a 4 x 2-inch piece of 1" x ½" 14-gauge *welded* mesh which is held in an open or "set" position by the top edge of the wire loop when the loop is made to engage one of the protruding cross rods of the welded mesh. The twisted "tail" made when forming the wire loop engages the inside of the front panel of the box just below the entrance hole.

(from *Wisconsin Bluebird*, March 1989.)

Huber Sparrow Trap

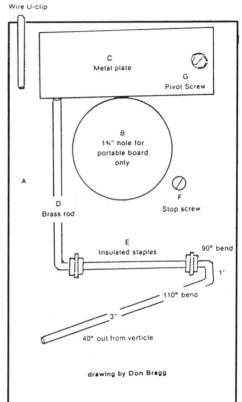

Wire U-clip

C
Metal plate

G
Pivot Screw

B
1¾" hole for
portable board
only

A

D
Brass rod

F
Stop screw

E
Insulated staples

90° bend

1"

110° bend

3"

40° out from verticle

drawing by Don Bragg

Either a portable or permanent Huber sparrow trap can be built from these instructions. The letters refer to corresponding letters on the drawing.

A. For the portable trap, cut a 4"x8½" piece of plywood (or a size that will fit your bird house).
B. For the portable trap, bore a 1¾" hole to give you a little leeway when aligning the trap hole with your bluebird nest box hole.
C. Steel plate 1¼"x3"x⅛" thick.
D. Brass rod or coat hanger wire bent to use as the trigger. Joe calls it the "trip rod."
E. Insulated electrical staples to mount the trip rod on the box and act as a hinge.
F. Stop screw (½" #6 round head wood screw).
G. Pivot screw (½" #6 round head screw or slotted hex head screw).

Additionally, a U-shaped clip made out of the same wire as the trigger works well to hold the portable trap board in position inside of a top opening box. The span of the clip equals the combined thickness of the box front and the portable trap boards.

For side opening boxes, a wood screw driven through the front of the box will engage the trap board to hold it in position.

To install the trip rod, measure down four inches and draw a line. This is where the trip rod is attached with the two insulated staples. The rod must be bent to shape before attaching.

Steps to follow: Attach the trap plate, then the stop screw, followed by the trip rod.

After completing the portable trap version, be sure to turn it over and file off the points of the staples and screws flush that may have penetrated the board to the other side.

Remember, this is a two dimensional drawing that does not show the three dimensional shape of the trip rod. You are forming the trip rod to be contacted by the sparrow's body when the bird drops into the lower box area.

When bluebirds are using the box and the trap is "at rest", the lower portion of the trip rod is flat against the box front, while the upper portion will not interfere with the coming and going of the bluebird pair.

175

Mel Bolt Sparrow Trap

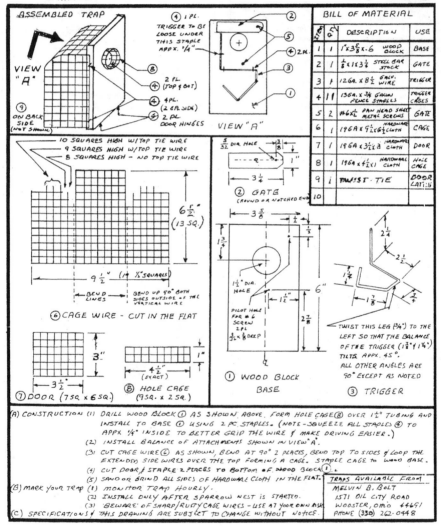

Ground Sparrow Traps

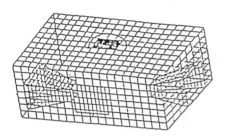

Tomahawk Sparrow Trap #501
Available from Tomahawk Live
Trap Company, P.O. Box 323,
Tomahawk, WI 54487. All wire
mesh; no moving parts. Birds enter
thru funnel at either end, cannot get
back out. Release door. Holds several sparrows at once, doesn't need
resetting. $52.43 plus shipping
1-800-272-8727

Three chamber wire sparrow trap.
Birds trrp lever on either side, hop
into middle space. Trap has to be
reset. Includes quick-release pole-
mounting bracket.Purple Martin
Conservation Association, Edinboro
University of Pennsylvania,
Edinboro, PA 16444. 814-734-4420.
e mail pmca@edinboro.edu
ST-1 Wire sparrow trap $32.95 +
$6 shipping.

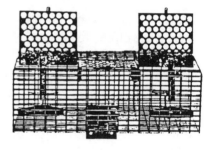

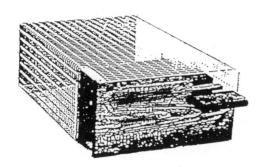

Cedar Valley Live Trap.
Sealed pine and wire. Ful-
crum trip lever. Hold several
birds at once. Raccoon &
squirrel proof. Access door.
Zell Olson Productions.
8128 Blaisdell Ave So.
Bloomington, MN 55420
$49.50 + $7.50 shipping.

Troyer Large Sparrow/Starling Trap

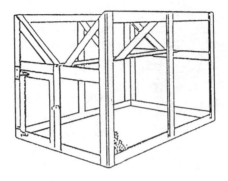

Various versions of this trap are available. Frame is of wood, with hardware cloth, screen, or 1" chicken wire. Starlings or sparrows drop down into open slot which runs across top. Bar below slot prevents them from flying out again. Holds many birds at once. Access door. A set of instructions is available for $6 from Andrew Troyer, Route 3, Box 72, Conneautville, PA 16401. Completed trap can be shipped: $254 plus $42.50 east of Mississippi River, $54.56 west of Mississippi.   1-800-872-0103

Also available: In-box Huber-Tuttle-Troyer Sparrow Trap, $6 plus $2.50 shipping and handling.

APPENDIX

Boz Metzdorf
Bird's Eye View Productions
1761 County Road H, Deer Park, WI 54007

Jewels of Blue. VHS 30 min.
Spectacular photography takes the viewer through the bluebird life cycle, with close-ups of courtship, nesting and care of young. Pioneer bluebirders interviewed.
$24.95 plus $2.00 shipping and handling for one, $2.40 for two.

Bluebird Trails. VHS 37 min.
Extremely informative video contains all necessary steps to learn bluebirding, starting and maintaining a trail, and dealing with predators and competitors. Beautiful photography.
$24.95 plus $2 S&H.

Backyard Blues. VHS 48 min.
Heart-warming depiction of bluebirds nesting in the backyard. Fledglings feeding at kitchen window and frolicing at bird bath. Bluebird orphans and more. Uplifting and entertaining.
$29.95 plus $2 S&H

(Wisconsin residents add 5% sales tax.)

179

MEALWORMS *(Tenebrio Molitor)*
HOW TO START AND MAINTAIN A "COLONY"
John Thompson

Mealworms are an excellent supplement to bird feeding as they provide additional protein to a bluebird's regular diet of 85% insects and 15% seeds, berries and fruit. When those early spring bluebirds arrive and insects are not abundant, the availability of mealworms in the vicinity of your bluebird nextboxes may be the difference between attracting bluebirds to your yard or having them move to a different area to begin their nesting activities.

In addition to Eastern, Western and Mountain Bluebirds, mealworms will attract a wide variety of popular bird feeder visitors. These birds, listed in the Midwest, LOVE mealworms:

American Robins	Chickadees	Juncos	Blackbirds
Fields Sparrows	Blue Jays	Mockingbirds	Grackels
Catbirds	Orioles	Purple Finches	Vireos
Downy Woodpeckers	Tanagers	Lazuli Buntings	Indigo Buntings
Hairy Woodpeckers	Purple Finches	Carolina Wrens	Song Sparrows
Northern Cardinals	Cowbirds	Warblers	Brown Creepers
Brown Thrashers	Kinglets		Nuthatches
Red-bellied Woodpeckers	Northern Cardinals		Rufus-sided Towhees
Rose-breasted Grosbeaks	Chipping Sparrows		Evening Grosbeaks

In other geographical areas an even greater variety of birds will be attracted to mealworms.

Mealworms are easy to raise. Only a few basics need to be followed to start and maintain a mealworm colony. Order regular size mealworms in bulk from a supplier, but be sure to keep them refrigerated. At room temperature the bran would be depleted and the worms would starve. Be sure to order regular size or fishing size. Giant or Jumbo sizes do not keep or reproduce well.

A 5 gallon plastic pail works well for the colony. Buy enough oat or wheat bran to half fill the pail. Bran is usually available in large food stores, or you may find it in feed stores. A year's supply will cost only a few dollars. When you receive your bulk mealworms they will be packed in crumpled newspaper. Shake the worms out of the paper into the pail. Put no more than 1,000 in one pail. If over-crowded they will generate heat and this will kill them. Keep them out of direct sunlight and avoid freezing. Preferable temperature is between 42 and 70 degrees. Occasionally, only about every two to three weeks, put in a few lettuce leaves, some apple or potato slices, or a banana peel. Put this food on a piece of cardboard or some paper towel. Never add moisture. As the mealworms consume the bran, a fine, dusty residue will settle to the lower portion of the pail. The uneaten top portion of the bran should be salvaged, along with the microscopic eggs, and the bottom portion should be discarded. Then half fill the pail with new bran. It shouldn't be necessary to do this more than about three times a year.

APPENDIX

The mealworms you receive from the supplier will be in the larval stage. They will cycle through 10 to 20 molts, into the pupa stage, and then into the adult beetle stage. The beetles are unable to fly, but beetles and worms can crawl, so you may want to cover the pail with a screen of some sort. Depending on food and temperature, these cyclic stages may last from 100 to several hundred days. Minute larvae will appear after the egg stage and these larvae will grow quite rapidly to the size you will use for your bird feeding. When my "colony" mealworms grow to a size comparable to the ones I received from the supplier, I remove some of them from the bran pail and put them in plastic containers with perforated covers and store them in the refrigerator. The coolness will keep them in the larval stage. Do not feed them apples, potatoes, etc. while they are refrigerated.

If I have a large reproduced quantity, I freeze some of them for future use. I feed them frozen to the winter bird feeder visitors, and they thrive on them. The frozen condition doesn't seem to bother the birds at all; they subsist on frozen food all winter long and are adapted to eating it. **But avoid supplying frozen worms when adults are feeding young birds in the nest, or feeding newly fledged birds.**

Special mealworm feeders are available, but not absolutely necessary. I use a small tin or plastic container placed in the vicinity of the bluebird activity, at first on the ground, and then fastened to the back of the nestbox after the birds come to recognize it as the food source. One to 1-1/2 dozen mealworms twice each day, for each bluebird pair, will keep them satisfied and not make them dependent on this supplement to their regular, natural diet. As the young birds are being fed in the nestbox and growing, you may want to increase the portions.

As a lure for photography, mealworms are a perfect accessory for getting close-up pictures. There are many excellent bluebird pictures that attest to this technique.

Nestboxes, mealworms, bird baths, short grass, scattered perching sites, regular monitoring, and protection from predators will provide you with unlimited enjoyment of "The bird that carries the sky on its back," as well as many other delightful songbirds.

Sources of mealworms

Rainbow Mealworms
P.O. Box 4907
126 E. Spruce St.
Compton, CA 90220
1-800-777-9676
2000/ $9.75 + airmail
1000/ $6.25 + $3

Grubco Mealworms
P.O. Box 15001
Hamilton, OH 45015
1-800-222-3563
1000/ $5 + $4.40

Sunshine Mealworms
Box 360
Silverton, OR 97381
1-800-322-1100
1000/ $6 + shipping

Southeastern Insectaries
(formerly Georgia Mealies)
606 Ball St.
Perry, GA 31069
1-877-967-6777 (toll free)
1000/ $6 + $3.20

181

BBRP ANNUAL REPORT FORM (1999)

BLUEBIRD REPORT FORM -- 1999

Note: If you had boxes in more than one county, please submit a separate report for each county.

*

last name	first name	box location: county	state

(   ) -

address	state	zip	telephone	e-mail (optional)

How many bluebird boxes did you monitor? _____

How often do your check your trail(s)? _____

How many boxes were occupied by bluebirds? _____

How many successful broods (a single nesting with one or more bluebirds fledged)? _____

How many bluebird eggs did you have — blue and/or white? _____

How many hatched? (this cannot be greater than the # of eggs) _____

How many fledged? (this cannot be greater than the # of eggs or hatched) _____

How many bluebird boxes did wrens try to use? _____ use successfully? _____
What method(s) were used to discourage wrens? _____

How many boxes did house sparrows try to use? _____ use successfully?_____

How many bluebird boxes were used successfully by tree swallows? _____
If tree swallows nested, were boxes paired? yes __ average distance between paired boxes? ___ not paired ___

How many boxes were used by chickadees? _____ others ? _____ (Note species)

If cat/raccoon protection was used on the pole, did it work?   yes ____ no ___
    What type of protection was on the pole? ___ grease ___1/2"-1&1/2 " pipe ___baffle ___none

If cat/raccoon protection was used at the entrance hole, did it work?   yes ____ no ___
    What type of protection was used at the hole? ___ wire guard ___2x4 wood block ___plastic ___none

Did you have any special problems? _____
_____

Please circle type & no. of nest boxes used by bluebirds:	A	B	C	D (PVC-plastic)	E Other
	X	X	X	X	X ....

Please return this form by **September 15, 1999** if you wish to be included in and receive the 1998
BLUEBIRD DIRECTORY. Return to BBRP / Scriven, 2044 Cedar Lake Pkwy, Mpls, MN 55416

Original BBRP Annual Report Form
(Optional Back side of report)

BBRP ANNUAL REPORT FORM – Detailed Data, Side 2

(OPTIONAL)
EXPANDED BLUEBIRD DATA FORM
****

DATA YEAR _____   DATE OF FIRST ARRIVAL _____

	HOUSE 1	HOUSE 2	HOUSE 3	HOUSE 4	HOUSE 5
DATE OF NESTING (first egg)					
NUMBER OF EGGS – Blue					
White					
DATE FLEDGED					
NUMBER FLEDGED					
TYPE OF MOUNT (wood, steel, other)					
TYPE OF HOUSE (BOX) (see types below – A,B,etc)					
COLOR OF HOUSE (BOX) (natural, painted – color)					
HEIGHT OF HOLE (feet)					
SIZE OF HOLE (1½, 2, 1 3/8 x 2¼, etc)					
DIRECTION OF HOLE (N, E, SW, etc)					
DISTANCE TO NEAREST BLUEBIRD HOUSE OCCUPIED BY A BLUEBIRD					
FOOD SOURCE (pasture, lawn, etc)					
DISTANCE TO FEEDING AREA					
DISTANCE TO PROTECTIVE COVER					
DISTANCE TO OUT BUILDINGS					
DISTANCE TO NEAREST HUMAN HOUSE					
DISTANCE TO NEAREST ROAD					
AMOUNT OF VEHICLE TRAFFIC (light to heavy)					
KIND OF SOIL (sand, loam, clay, etc)					
DISTANCE TO WATER (lake, stream, etc)					

IS THE TOTAL NUMBER OF BLUEBIRDS MORE, SAME or LESS THAN LAST YEAR _____

A   B   C   D   E Other
                       (specify)

A Sampling of Letters from Bluebirders

From New Richland, Minnesota,

Dear Mrs. Scriven,

In March I received a letter from you explaining some of the details of starting a "Bluebird Trail." My son Brent agreed that a bluebird trail would be a fun learning experience and decided to use his bluebird trail as a 4-H project. We put up five bluebird nesting boxes on May 14th. May 19th we saw a pair of bluebirds. What a thrill for the whole family. For me it was the first time I ever saw a bluebird! Shortly after our bluebirds made a nest in house No.1.

By June 3rd there were four bluebird eggs in house No.~1. By June 14th we saw four little "plucked chickens". Bluebirds may not be the most beautiful babies in the world but they were beautiful to us. By June 26th we could tell they would soon be ready to fly. June 29th we saw the lot of them setting on the hi-line wires. We all had sad and yet warm feelings about seeing them leave the nest.

Brent's 4-H project was a real success. He did several things in relationship to his project. First off he gave a demonstration to his local 4-H club. I felt he did so well that I encouraged him to give a demonstration at the Waseca Co.County Fair. This also gave him a really good opportunity to tell others of the problems bluebirds have and how people all over can help. What a success he had with his demonstration. He received a blue ribbon and later received reserve champion. Quite an honor for a 10-year-old when the competition is great. The very very best part though was the response of the audience. They were asking questions; they even came up afterwards. It was just so neat seeing the interest shown by others in starting a bluebird trail.

Brent also entered the conservation division at the fair. He built a 6th house, took the bluebird nest out of house 31, made clay eggs, labeled the house explaining the important features. He also made a poster book telling the bluebirds' story. He also had his records to show. It was a lot of work, but he was really thrilled when he won 'grand champion' in conservation at the fair.

184

He's too young yet to go to the state fair because of his awards, but he said the best award was knowing he helped make more bluebirds.

Oh, I just about forgot! We got PG again! Low and behold, July 19th we checked house No.~1 and there were 4 more bluebird eggs!!! This batch hatched out within the next few weeks and left the nest on August 3rd. So we can report a total of eight new baby bluebirds in this world. We sure hope some return next year. We're going to put up five more houses. By the way, house No.3 hatched out five little tree swallows.

This project has not only been rewarding for my son, but it's been rewarding for my whole family. Personally I can no longer walk through a woods or drive down a road without looking to see the birds. I've just become so much more aware. One of the funnest days I spent was an afternoon that I decided to get a picture of the bluebirds for Brent's 4-H project. Do you know I laid out in the weeds (covered up with weeds and everything) for 2-1/2 hours to get a picture. At the time I was disgusted that they were so shy, but I sure did learn a lot watching them. The pictures turned out so well that I now look at the experience as rewarding. Our 4-H club is thinking of taking up bluebirds as a club project and several friends would like to start a trail, too. Would it be possible to send me 12 copies of the pamphlet called 'Help Bring Back our Gems
of Blue'?

Another question — should bluebird nests be removed at the end of season? As I mentioned, we removed the bluebirds' first nest after ten days because we figured they wouldn't nest again. But they rebuilt and did soon after we removed it. What have others found out?

Our bluebirds seemed impressed because our houses were made out of lumber that we saved when we tore down an old house. The wood was extra thick (1 to 1-1/2") and has an old smell and look.
Hope you'll be able to send the pamphlets.

Sincerely,

Mrs.Richard Possin

From Shafer, Minnesota, September 12, 1988:

Dear Mary Ellen,

Raising two baby bluebirds is quite insignificant, but what a joy to watch the parents, their two fledged babies from the first batch and then the two raised in the box in our yard. We used several methods to chase sparrows away, all unsuccessful! I almost shot holes in the roof of our metal pole shed. I'm sure people driving by must have laughed watching me chase sparrows with a broom. I hope, when I chased with the water hose, people thought I was watering the lawn. We still had four bluebirds in the birdbaths yesterday, Sept.~11.

Thank you for the info about bluebirds. We've never had bluebirds nest in the yard in thirty years until this summer.

Sincerely,

Helen Sellman

From Chisago City, Minnesota, August 27, 1988:

Dear Dorene,

One subject that we didn't see mentioned in the list of things that you will talk about in the book is the trail operator's relationship with the landowners where the houses are.

For us, we really enjoy the long distance wave across the pasture or field — a welcome feeling. Each winter we renew our request to keep the houses on their farms for another year. This is always answered with 'by all means, keep those houses on my land' — some tell me that we are always welcome and to 'roam anywhere you want.'

In December we write each landowner a letter telling of this year's results on their farm and on others, making a point to mention a special location that produced a brood of bluebird on their 'fence by the creek.'

We include a township plot map with our whole trail system laid out in color for each farmer to see our overall coverage of neighboring farms. We include a small Wildlife Picture Calendar and a 'Bird' Christmas card with our special 'thank you so very much for the use of your beautiful land.' This is an enjoyable way for us to keep in touch with those people who have all that perfect bluebird habitat.

It brings us great joy to be pointed out and spoken of as the bluebird people by those farmers when we meet them in town or at the voting booth. We really value our relationships with these people as we have some of the most beautiful walking trails in the state for free.

We notice this very same special relationships between\<Al Dawson> and Russ Krause with their landowners that long distance wave and followed up with a chat of 'how you doing today.'

I think I like the statement one farmer made years ago best of all — 'You're wasting your time — bluebirds were here when I was a boy — but they're all gone now.' That next spring I counted 24 in the pasture across from his home and I can see them any time I look now in the pines around his house.

We have the utmost respect for these lands we walk on. We pick up any cans or bottles, just to make it a bit better for the cows, when we leave. This is a very pleasing hobby to have — thanks, Dorene, for being one who shared it with us.

Yours truly,

Dick and Marlys Hjort

[Part of an article by Harry Krueger, Texas, reprinted by Keith Kridler via e-mail March 18, 1999]

" The personal satisfaction and pleasure derived by participating in monitoring nestboxes is a reward money cannot buy. Whether you have one box or fifty, the joy and excitement of seeing a new nest, then blue eggs and observing the nestlings, is almost beyond description. Observing bluebirds in the nestbox is a celebration of life — one of the many miracles afforded us in this world." -- Harry Krueger

Letter attached to the 1997 BBRP report form of Allison McCormick, Royal Oak, Michigan [edited version)]. (Allison took over the monitoring of Katie Kurtagh's trail in Livingston County.)

"Life is a series of choices and one such choice I made on April 10, 1996 has immeasurably enriched my life. An unusually cold but sunny Saturday morning had me leaning towards staying home with an extra cup of coffee and "This Old House". But something prodded me out the door to Island Lake Recreation Area where an Oakland Audubon field trip, focusing on a "bluebird trail", was being held. The short version of the rest of the story is that I was enchanted by the bluebirds and had immediate affection and admiration for Katie Kurtagh, a retired nurse, who was the trail monitor. Katie accepted my offer to volunteer my time to her trail and invited me along on one of her monitoring days. I was captivated and continued my visits. As they say, "timing is everything" and since Katie had been searching for a replacement, she offered the opportunity to me. I am honored and grateful for the chance to continue her legacy and will work hard to maintain the conscientious standards she has set for the trail. In no way has Katie abandoned the trail, she continues to make weekly visits and offers indispensable guidance. My utmost gratitude to you, Katie.

"1997 was my first year as a bluebird trail monitor and record keeper. I have a new awareness for the diligence and attention necessary to create an accurate and complete report. My attachment to each of the boxes has strengthened, and I have a heightened sense of responsibility to each of the avian families inhabiting them. I understand the significance of properly recording their life histories....

*"As I have said to Katie, I don't know what I did without bluebirds in my life? Ahh, but they are here now and if Katie's longevity * is any indicator, I won't be looking for my replacement for another 40 years."*

*Ed's note: Katie is an octogenarian.

It is much more logical, efficient, and cost effective
to preserve a species from declining
than to manage population recovery.

Carrol Henderson

If the warble of the first bluebird does not thrill you,
know that the morning and spring of your life
are past.

Henry David Thoreau

NOTES

Bibliography

Ahlgren, Dave. 1984ff. Directories of the Bluebird Recovery
    Program of Minnesota, 1984-88.
Aylesworth, Art. Personal communications to DHS, Dec. 1998
    — March 1999
- - - 12/10/97. NABS approved nest boxes. Fowarded letter to Kevin
    Berner.
Arnett, Ross H. & Richard Jacques, Jr. 1981Simon & Schuster's
    Guide to Insects.

Baer, Bruce. 2/6/96. Prothonotary warbler locations. Internet: MIN
    NESOTA BIRDING
Baker, R. Robin. 1984. Bird Migration —The Solution of a Mystery?
    Homes & Meir, New York.
Barbin, Diane. 2/22/99.[Bauldry box] Internet: BLUEBIRD-L
Beimborn, Donald A. 1967. Population Ecology of the English
    Sparrow (*Passer domesticus*) in North America. Master's Thesis,
    Univ. Wisconsin, Milwaukee
Beimborn, Donald A. 1976. Sex ratios in the English Sparrow:
    Sources of Bias. *Bird Banding* 47(1):13-18
Bent, Arthur Cleveland. 1949. Life Histories of North American
    Thrushes, Kinglets and Their Allies. Dover, N.Y., p. 235ff
Berner, Kevin L. 1990. Field tests of predator-deterrent nest box
    devices for acceptance by cavity nesting birds. *Sialia* 12(4)123
- - - and Veronica A. Pleines. 1993. Field tests of several styles of
    bluebird nest boxes. *Sialia* 15(1):3-10
- - - 1995. Comparison of use of several styles of nest boxes by
    cavity-nesting birds: an update. BBRP Research Grant

- - - 1998. Observations on pairing bluebird nest boxes. *Sialia* 20(2) 49-50
- - - Research Report, NABS Board Meeting, Oct. 24-25, 1998. Madison, WI.
Bonta, Marcia. Tufted Titmouse. Jan/Feb 1999. *Bird Watcher'sDigest,* p. 24
Boone, D. Daniel. 1988. Bluebird, What Do You Eat? *Sialia.* Anniversary Issue: p. 9
Bower, Allen. Britton, MI. Personal Communication 8-16-98. Personal communication 4-12-99
Bragg, Don. 2/2/99.Horizontal nestboxes. Internet: BLUEBIRD-L
Brunell, Dr. Shirl. 1984. I Hear Bluebirds. Coltrane and Beach, Los Angeles.
Bryan & Pease, Agricultural Pesticides& Wildlife — A Balancing Act. Iowa State Univ. Ext.Service USFW Bulletin
Bryan, James R. 1988. Radio-controlled Bow-Net for American Kestrels. *North American Bird Bander* XIII(12):30

Campbell, Ira. 1982. Experimental Nesting Box Designed to Reduce Blowfly Parasitism. *Sialia* 4(2):49
- - - 1984. Experimental Design to Reduce Blowfly Parasitism. *Sialia* 6(2):70
Canadian Wildlife Service, 1994.Technical Report Series #202 Burlington, Ontario.
Carson, Rachel. 1962. Silent Spring. Houghton-Mifflin, Boston
Chance, Paul. 1996. The elevator post .*Sialia* 18(2):63
Churcher, J.B. & J.H. Lawton. 1987. *J. Zool.Lond.* 212:439-455
Cook, Jim, Germantown, MD. 7-30-98. Personal e-mail to DHS.
Cousineau, Michelle & Welsey Moore. 1986. Comparison of an Established Bluebird Trail to New Trails. *Sialia* 8(3):83

Darling, Christopher & Julia Thompson-Delaney. 1992. Bluebirds, Blowflies, and Parasitic Wasps. *Rotunda* 25(1):37-40
Davis, Wayne H. 1989. House sparrows prefer a circular entrance. *Sialia* 11(1):8
- - - 1995. Testing the features of the Peterson box. *Sialia* 17(4): 135

- - - 1995. Tests of the Peterson & Zuern's Tree Branch box.. *Sialia* 17(1):18
- - - & Wm.McCom. 1988. Use of Tangle Trap to Measure Snake Predation at Bluebird Boxes. *Sialia* 10(3):82-88
Dew, Tina & R. B. Leighton. 1986. Bluebirds — Their Daily Lives and How to Attract and Raise Bluebirds. Nature Book Publishers, Jackson, MI
Droeges,Sam,9-29-94 Eastern Bluebird Trends.Internet: BIRDCHAT .

Efta, Rita. 1989. Review notes to DHS
Eno, Steve. 1998. Troyer box report. *Bluebirds Across Nebraska* 5(3)

Fiedler, Carol. 1988. Research Paper presented at 1988 BBRP Conference, St. John's University
- - - 1999. Personal correspondence to DHS
Fielder, David. 1974. Ecology of the Eastern Bluebird in Central Minnesota. Master's Thesis, St. Cloud State University.
- - - Eight Year Study following Master's Thesis
Finch, Jack. 1994 . Is There a Need to Feed Bluebirds? (Revised Pamphlet)
- - - June 16 1998. Demonstration, NABS Annual Conference, Regina, Saskatchewan
Fitz, Ken. 1995. Nestbox preferences. *Dawes Arboretum Newsletter*, March

Gilbertson, Steve. 1990-1999. Personal communications to DHS
Gillis, Earl. 1985. Personal Communcation. Survival Temperatures [of western blubebirds]

Gowaty, P.A. 1981. Aggression of breeding eastern bluebirds towards their mates and models of intra- and interspecific intruders. *Animal Behavior* 29 1013-1027.
- - - 1983. Male parental care and apparent monogamy among eastern bluebirds.*The American Naturaist.*121(2):149-157
- - - 1984. Multiple Maternity and Paternity in Single Broods of Apparently Monogamous Eastern Bluebirds. *J. Field Ornithology.* 55:378-380

- - - and A.A. Karlin. 1984. House Sparrows Kill Eastern Bluebirds. *Behavioral Ecology and Sociobiology* 15:91-95
- - - and D.W.Mock,eds. Avian Monogamy. *Ornithol. Monogr.* 37
- - - and William C. Bridges. 1991.Nestbox availability affects extra-pair fertilization and conspecific nest parasitism in eastern bluebirds. *Ann. Biol.* 41:661-675
- - - and Jonathan Plissner. 1997. Breeding dispersal of eastern bluebirds depends on nesting success but not on removal of old nests: an experimental study. *J.FIeld Ornithol.* 68(3)323-502
- - - and Jonathan Plissner. 1998. Eastern Bluebird. The Birds of North America. No. 381
Graham, Hatch.. 1997. Are we leading our predators to our nest boxes? *Bluebirds Fly,* (Newsl. CA Bluebird Recovery Program,) *Vol. 3(2):* 2
- - - 1997. Western bluebird decline continues in California. *Ibid* 3(3):3
- - - 1999. Monitoring Guide- — Monitoring Your Bluebird Trail in California. 3rd, Ed. (Pamphlet)
- - - 1999. Spotlight on our cavity nesters: Oak Titmouse. *Bluebirds Fly.* 5 (1):3
Guinan, Judith. Jan-March 1999. Personal communications with DHS
- - - 1999: Western Bluebirds. The Birds of North America. [In print]
Grant, George. 1988. Which nesting box should I use? *Sialia,* Tenth Anniversary Issue., p. 11
Grussing, Don. 1980. How to Trap House Sparrows. Roseville Publishing House, Roseville, MN

Hagerman, Donna. 1988. Nesting box entrance hole size preferred by mountain bluebirds. *Sialia* 10(3):83-86
- - - 3/14 - 15, 1999. Personal communications to DHS
Hanes, Frances. 1984. Emergency aid for bluebirds. *Sialia* 6(1):18
Hartshorne, James. M. 1962. Behavior of the eastern bluebird at the nest. *Living Bird, First Annual of the Cornell Laboratory of Ornithology.*pp 131-149. Ithaca, NY

Harwood, Garth. 1998. Meeting the challenge: a case for nestbox diversity. *Bluebirds Fly* (Newsl of CA Bluebird Rec. Prog.) 4(2):5

Havera, S. and N. Havera. 1983. Kestrels prey on nestling bluebird. *Sialia* 5(3):93

Henderson, Carrol. 1988a. Landscaping For Wildlife. MN. Dept. Natural Resources, St. Paul, MN

- - - 1988b. Current Ornithology. Ed: Richard Johnston. Vol.5, Chapt.7, p.297

- - - 1992.Woodworking For Wildlife. MN. Dept. Natural Resources, St. Paul, MN

Hineman, Julie. Sept. 9, 1998. Personal communication to DHS

Hill, Jaclyn. 1990 ff. personal communcations to DHS.

Hill, James J.III. 1988. Editor, *Purple Martin Update* 1(2)May

Huber, Joe. 1988. Person communication to DHS

- - - April 11,1999 Personal communication to DHS

Humbla, Svante. 1980 - 1999.Personal communications to DHS

Janilla, Linda. 1/29/99& 1/30/99. [cracked eggs.] Personal e-mail to DHS

Johnson, Vern. 1998. White-breasted nuthatch. *The Nestbox* (Newsl. So. Inter. Bluebird Trail. Soc., British Columbia. 7. Spring

Johnston, Pat. 12/16/97. Personal communciation to DHS

Kingston, Ron. 1991. Ron Kingston's snake/predator guard. *Sialia* 13(2):56-57

Kridler, Keith. 1988. Are PVC nest boxes sparrow resistant? *Sialia* 10(1):3

- - - Feb, 1, 1999.[Electro-magnetic field s and fire ants] Internet: BLUEBIRD-L

- - - 2/11/99. PVC/heat. *Ibid*

Krueger, Harry. 1988. A carbaryl pesticide suspected in the death of nestlings. *Sialia* 10(3):93

- - - 1989. Fire ant solution. *Ibid* 11(1)27

Lehmann., D.M. 1997. Controlled tests to determine if European Starlings can pass through various holes sizes. *Sialia* 19(4)

Leonard, Marty et. al. 1994. Provisioning in western bluebirds is not
    related to offspring sex. *Behavorial Ecology* 5(4):455-459
Losure, Mary. 1997. Odyssey of the house finch. *Bird Watcher's
    Digest* Sept-Oct. p.45

Malone, Howard Jan 6.1999. [Feeding cottonseed meal to bluebirds]
    Internet: BLUEBIRD-L
Mauritz, Marilyn. 1980. (Letter to the Editor). *Minnesota Bird Bander*
    22:9
McComb, W.C., W.H. David & P.N. Allaire. 1987. Excluding star-
    lings. *Wildlife Society Bulletin* 15::204-220
Mundahl, Neal. 1993. BBRP Research Grant.(Nestbox temperatures)
Musselman. 1934. *Bird Lore* 36:1

National Geographic Society. 1988 Field Guide to the Birds of North
    America. 2nd Ed.
Navratil, Frank.1998. Nest cavity temperature vs. nest box color.
    (Document)
- - - 1998. Floyd Kudla's success with hanging nest boxes on urban
    trails. *Sialia* 20(2):62
Niebuhr, Robert M. 2/19/1999. Box placement & pairing. Internet:
    BLUEBIRD-L

Orthwein, Bob. 1996a. An experimental house wren guard.
- - - 1996b. Triple box locations are stills saving bluebirds and tree
    swallows from house sparrow attacks. *Bluebird Monitor*
    (News.l. Ohio Bluebird Soc.) 11(5):4
Ostfeld, Richard S. 1997. The ecology of Lyme-disease risk. *Ameri-
    can Scientist* 85, pp. 338-346.

Palahniuk & Eugene B. Bakko. 1995. Nesting activity on a paired-
    box trail. *Sialia* 17(1): 3
Parren, Steven G. Orientation and spacing of nesting boxes used by
    eastern bluebirds and tree swallows. *Sialia* 16(4) 127-129
Pearman, Myrna. 1992. Nestboxes for Prairie Birds. Ellis Bird Farm,
    LTD, Alberta.

- - - 1998. Mountain bluebird recoveries south of the 49th parallel. *Ellis Bird Farm Newsletter. 12(1)3*

- - - 1999 Personal communications to DHS

- - - 1999. NABS Entrance Hole Study (chart)

Peterson, Dick. 1979 - 1999. Personal communications to DHS

Peterson, Roger Tory. 1980. A Field Guide to the Birds.Houghton-Mifflin. Publ., Boston, MA

Pinkowski, Ben.C. 1975. Growth and development of eastern bluebirds. *Bird Banding* 46(4): 273-289

Plissner, Jonathan H. and Patricia A. Gowaty. 1988. Evidence of reproductive error in adoption of nestling eastern bluebirds. *The Auk.* 105(3) 575-577

- - - Sept. 1995.Presentation to the Bluebird Recovery Program, Minnesota, Conference

Power, Harry W. & Michael P. Lombardo. 1996, Mountain Bluebird. The Birds of North America. No. 222

Prescot, Hubert and Earl Gillis. 1985. An Analysis of western bluebird double and triple nest box reseatch on Chehalem and Parrett Mountains in 1982. *Sialia* 7(4): 123-130.

Price, Jeanne. 1982. Presidential Points. *Sialia* 4(3):82

Purvis, Dick. 1997. Hanging Nest Box. *Sialia* 19(4)144

- - - 1997. Cavity nester success in Orange County, CA *Sialia* 19(4)143

- - - 4/14/99. Hanging boxes. Internet: BLUEBIRD-L

- - - 1/16/99. Berries. *Ibid*

- - - May 4, 1999. Wrens. *Ibid*

- - - Feb.22, 1999. Bewick's Wren. *Ibid.*

Read, William F. 1988. Excerpt in No. American Bird Bander 13(2):53-54.

Roberts, Thomas F. 1932. Birds of Minnesota. Vol. 2., Univ. MN Press, Minneapolis

Robbins, Chandler, B. Bruun & N.Zim. 1984. Birds of North America. Golden Press, 1984.

Romaner, Jean. 3/9/99. Monitoring aid. Internet: BLUEBIRD-L

Rustad, Orwin. 1972. An Eastern bluebird nesting study in South Central Minnesota. The Loon 44(3):80-841972-1999

- - - 1979-1999 First arrival dates. Personal communcations to DHS

Sawyer, Laurance. 1988. *Nat. Soc. News* 23(10):6

Schaefer, E. J. 1992. Personal communication to DHS

Sedlacek, Joseph R. 1988. Experimenting with raccoon guards. *Sialia* 9 (3): 83-85

Shantz, Bryan R. and Myrna Pearman. 1984. Nest Boxes for Alberta Birds. Ellis Bird Farm, LTD, Alberta

- - - 1986a. A History of the Ellis Bird Farm. *Sialia* 8(4) 143-146.

- - - 1986b. Mountain Bluebird Management. (Pamphlet- 32 pp.) Deer Ridge Consulting Ltd, & NABS

Sillick, Darlene. 1/27/99. Blowflies, Rotenone. Internet: BLUE BIRD-L

- - - 4/23/99. Nesting material— nest I.D. Internet: BLUE BIRD-L

Sims, Richard A. Fire ant predation on blowfly larvaein a bluebird nestbox. *Sialia* 17(1):96

Sprenger, Jack. 9/9/94. Comments on branch box. Personal communication to DHS

Stave, DarrellW. 6/25/98. Personal communication to DHS

Steffen. 1981. Unusual hunting behavior of the American kestrel. *Inland Bird Banding* 53(3):54-55

Stiles, Donald. 1995ff. *Calgary Area Bluebird Trails.*

Teale, EdwinWay. 1974. A Naturalist Buys a Farm.p. 64-65. Dodd Mead & Co., NY

- - - 1978. A Walk Through the Year. Dodd Mead & Co., NY

- - - 1954. The Wilderness World of John Muir. [Chapter: A Paradise of Birds] p. 35. Houghton Mifflin, Boston.

Terres. John K. 1980. The Audubon Society Encylopedia of
    North American Birds. Alfred A. Knopf. New York

Thomas, Owen A. 3/22/99. Maynard's Diazinon Question.
    Internet: BLUEBIRD-L

Toops. Connie. 1994. Bluebirds Forever. Voyageur Press,
    Stillwater, MN

- - - 1995. Friendly competition. Birder's World. June 1995. p.
    16

Troyer, Andy. 1999. Bring Back the Bluebirds. (Pamphlet)

Tuttle, Richard M. 1991. An analysis of the interspecific compe-
    tition of eastern bluebirds, tree swallows, and house
    wrens in Delaware State Park, Ohio, 1979-1986. *Sialia*
    13(1) 3-13

Tschida, Jerry. 1989, Personal communciation to DHS

Valdiva, Jenny. 1998. Combating avian predators at nest boxes.
    Newsl. Prescott Western Bluebird Recovery Project.
    8(2):2

Violett, Linda. 3/10/99. Hooked on hangers. Internet: BLUE
    BIRD-L

Weaver, R.L. [Many articles on English Sparrows]. Bird Band-
    ing. *Wilson Bulletin*, Canada

Weidner, Robert. 1990. Chilled egg phenomenon. *Wisconsin
    Bluebird* (Newsl. BRAW) 5(3):1-2

Williams, Jim., Ed. 1996. Finding Eurasian tree sparrows in
    Iowa. *MN Birding*. Jan-Feb. p. 12

Willis, Don 1988. Prothonotary warbler recovery. Eastern
    Ontario Bluebird Society. pp 7-8

Wilson, Bob 1/7/99. Free material for nestboxes.Internet:
    BLUEBIRD-L

- - - 2/10/99. Gilbertson boxes. *Ibid*

- - - 5/3/99. MOBL holesize.*Ibid*

Zeleny, Lawrence. 1969. Starlings versus native cavity nesting birds. *Atlantic Naturalist* 24(3): 158-161

- - - 1976. The Bluebird - How You Can Help Its Fight for Survival. Indiana Univ. Press, Bloomington

- - - 1983. The remarkable process of incubation. *Sialia* 5(3): 108-109.

- - - 1986. The bluebird's parasitic blowfly. *Sialia* 8(4):136-138

- - - 1988. Can oprhanied bluebird nestlings and abandoned eggs be saved? *Sialia* 10(1):7-8

Zickefoose, Julie. 1993. Enjoying Bluebirds More. [Pamphlet - Bird Watcher's Digest, Marietta, OH

- - - 1997. In the company of bluebirds.. *Bird Watcher's Digest* Sept/Oct. p. 28

- - - 1998. Winterizing your bird boxes. *Bird Watcher's Digest* Sept/Oct. pp. 86-90

Zyla, John & Mike Donovan. 1993.Prothonotary warblers use nestbox inside capital gateway. *Sialia* 15(1): 20-22

Index

INDEX

preference, 50
sources, 169ff
spacing, 63
  wren guard, 115
nesting sites, 22
nestlings, 30-32, 92, 95 - 97
  abandonment, 164
  fostering, 99- 100, 166
  hand-raising, 162-163
  orphaned, 164
Niebuhr, Bob 9, 64
Nissen, Lois, 7
Noel, Jim, 79
Noel predator guard, *see* predator
                    guard, Noel
North American Bluebird Society,
  see NABS
numbering, of nest boxes, 91
nuthatch, 118 - 119, 153

opossums, 143
orphaned bluebirds, 162
Ortiz, Jo Ellen, 7

painting, of nest boxes, 44
pairing, of nest boxes, 13, 21, 63-66
parasites, 25, 143ff
parentage, mixed, 13
Parren, Steve G., 65
Passer domesticus, see house
                    sparrow
peanut hearts, 164
perches, 35, 81-82
PermaKill®, 107
Permanone® 107
permethrin, 144
pesticides, 19, 144, 150, 152, 156
Peterson, Dick, 6, 8, 11, 25, 34,

50, 148
Peterson, Vi, 6,
physical characteristics, 14
pine needles, 25
pipe, 71, 73, 76
  downspout, 76-77
  PVC, 45, 71-72, 76-77
  stovepipe, 77
plantings, 157ff
plastic, in nest, 120
plastic nest box, 44
polyvinyl chloride, *see* PVC
populations
  bluebird, 19
Possin, Brent, 184-185
Possin, Mrs. Richard, 184-185

posts
  metal, 70
  natural, 69
  separate, 69
  sign, 70
  utility, 69
  wooden, 69
predation, *see* predators
predator guard, 74-75, 78-80
  climbing, 73-75
  cones, 76-77
  exterior, 79,-80
  Jensen-Arndt, 75
  Noel, 79080, 173
  plastic, 80
  sheet metal, 75, 76
  wire, 78 - 79
  wooden, 78
  Zeleny, 75
predators, 127—142
  climbing, 50, 138—142
  summary, 151- 153

205

About the Editor

Given freedom to roam in an extensive wildlife preserve next to her childhood home south of San Francisco, Dorene Scriven early developed a love of nature. After graduating from the University of California at Berkeley in biological sciences, her marriage, three children, and her husband's university career took her to the East Coast, back to Berkeley, and finally to Minneapolis in 1959.

Until 1989 she worked part-time as a medical editor, personal secretary, and newsletter editor. A charter member of the Bluebird Recovery Program of the National Audubon Chapter of Minneapolis, she chaired that program from 1981 to 1987 and returned as chair in 1993. The Bluebird Recovery Program of Minnesota has 1300 members in 48 states and abroad. Dorene also is a Board Member of the North American Bluebird Society, and member of the NABS *Bluebird* Advisory Committee and the Technical Advisory Committee.

Dorene maintains, year-round, a 119-acre wildlife preserve adjacent to Lake Maria State Park in Central Minnesota, where she monitors, with the help of volunteers, 120 bluebird nestboxes.